Then There Was

Light

Then There Was Light

Stories Powered By The Rural Electrification Scheme In Ireland

WITHDRAWN

PJ Cunningham — EDITORS — **Dr Joe Kearney**

Ballpoint Press

*This book is dedicated to all those who had
a role in the electrification of Rural Ireland*

Published in 2016 by Ballpoint Press
4 Wyndham Park, Bray, Co Wicklow, Republic of Ireland.
Telephone: 00353 86 821 7631
Email: ballpointpress1@gmail.com
Web: www.ballpointpress.ie

ISBN 978-0-9954793-1-9

While every effort has been made to ensure the accuracy of
all information contained in this book, neither the author
nor the publisher accepts liability for any errors or omissions made.

Book design and production by Joe Coyle Media&Design,
joecoyledesign@gmail.com

© Cover photos and inside photographs, courtesy ESB Archives
Back cover: Painting by artist Eugene Conway, courtesy ESB Archives

Printed and bound by GraphyCems

Contents

Contents

Poems And Songs

Foreword

IT has been widely acknowledged that the Electricity Supply Board (ESB) was at the heart of arguably the greatest single change in Irish life brought about in the middle of the last century by "The Rural Electrification Scheme".

Seventy years later in 2016, it is indeed fitting that the stories surrounding that national roll-out should be recorded for posterity.

When we set about gathering some of those memories from former ESB workers in that scheme and people who witnessed the historic development along the highways and byways, little did we think there would be such a massive response from the general public as well.

While there was a lot of commonality in the accounts of gangs and poles arriving and later for the switching-on ceremonies, many amazing stories were sent to us, which are now being preserved for posterity in this collection.

We would like to record our appreciation to those who wrote their stories or were interviewed for this collection on the Rural Electrification Scheme.

Part of the tradition of Ireland has been our ability to comment on what's happening around us in song and verse. Accordingly, we have also included a section reflecting this heritage.

The hope is that the book in its entirety will provide a valuable snapshot of how the people of that time responded as the first tentative steps on the road to modern Ireland were taken.

PJ Cunningham — EDITORS — *Dr Joe Kearney*

Acknowledgements

W E would firstly like to record our sincere thanks to all the people who got in touch with the ESB and ourselves to make this publication possible.

Hundreds of people had either stories to tell or information to pass on which allowed us to produce both this book and an accompanying radio documentary.

We also are thankful that many of the vignettes from the time, while not suitable for this publication, are now also recorded, collated and safely preserved in the extensive ESB Archives for future generations of researchers, historians and sociologists.

Within the ESB this project was greeted with a warmth and enthusiasm that made this project a labour of love for the co-editors.

We are particularly indebted for the guidance and support of ESB Archives staff – Brendan Delany, Brian McMahon, Deirdre McParland and Kirsten Mulrennan.

This team plays a critical role in safeguarding the history and heritage of ESB and they do so with huge professionalism and passion. The archive was a very rich and invaluable source for our research where we also sourced virtually all of the photos that tell their own stories as part of this anthology.

We would like to record our gratitude to Bernadine Maloney, Corporate Communications and Public Affairs Manager, ESB and the company's Senior Press Officer, Paul Hand for the continuous enthusiasm they showed for this project from the outset.

Our thanks also to ESB CEO, Pat O'Doherty, for setting the scene for this book by writing the introduction.

Lastly, to our own families for the support they gave us while we were absent on this *Then There Was Light* mission that took up so much of 2016 – the 70th anniversary of the ESB's Rural Electrification Scheme.

EDITORS

Then There Was Light

Introduction

THE rural electrification scheme was one of the most important social and economic developments of 20th century Ireland. It transformed a very tough way of life that had existed for generations and sowed the seeds for Ireland's future growth and prosperity.

To understand its origins, it is necessary to go back to the Shannon Scheme which had been completed almost three decades earlier. Thomas McLaughlin, a young engineer who had worked with Siemens in Germany together with the senior executives of that company, convinced the new Irish Free State Government to invest one fifth of its annual revenue in a scheme to harness the flow of the Shannon to supply electricity to the nation.

McLaughlin passionately believed that electricity held the key to our economic development and recognised its potential to transform Ireland. At the time, the country was recovering from the aftermath of civil war and the First World War and life was difficult and uncertain. The Government shared McLaughlin's vision, realising that the completion of a major infrastructure project would be a potent symbol of political independence and economic sovereignty.

From the outset, McLaughlin was clear in his intent that Ireland's rural communities should enjoy the comforts that villagers in other lands took for granted, commenting later: "My country of which I was so intensely proud must not lag behind other lands... Electricity, the great key uplift of the country, must be provided on a national scale, cheap and abundant".

In developing the Shannon Scheme, the Government had accepted the premise that unified control of the production and distribution of electricity was necessary to achieve the rapid development Ireland needed. ESB was created in 1927 with full responsibility for the generation, transmission, distribution and marketing of electricity, thus becoming not only the first semi-state body in Ireland but also the first fully national electricity service in the world. Thomas McLaughlin was appointed as the first managing director.

Over the next two decades, ESB brought electricity to every major town and village in Ireland, taking over responsibility from local authorities and buying out private electricity suppliers. However although prices fell, electricity remained expensive and 400,000 homes remained without electricity.

In the 1930s, the Government's focus on economic development through self-sufficiency led to the creation of new semi-state bodies, including Bord na Móna, CIÉ and Irish Sugar. Within ESB, there was a steadfast belief that the development of a rural electricity network could further support this movement and would help to drive the country forward.

Thanks to the leadership and pioneering spirit of people like Thomas McLaughlin, William Roe and Paddy (PJ) Dowling in ESB, and the foresight of the political establishment at the time, the scheme was given the go ahead and work on the first phase began in 1946.

This was an enormous achievement. Cost was a major factor and, like today's deliberations around rural broadband which has the potential to be equally transformative, the Government had to be convinced that this was the right way to allocate scarce resources in the face of other political pressures.

The Rural Electrification Scheme was executed with what can only be described as patriotic zeal. William Roe who was in charge of the project and his deputy PJ Dowling were not only highly educated and experienced, but also hugely committed to Ireland's future. For many of the young workers involved, their own rural backgrounds and the opportunity to work on something truly innovative fuelled their passion to get the job done and the can-do attitude that came to characterise the scheme.

When I joined ESB in 1981, the sense of camaraderie and esprit de corps of the 'rural' group was still evident. They epitomised the close-knit teamwork that comes from years of helping each other out on the highways and byways of the country and left a lasting legacy for the company.

We talk a lot today of stakeholder management and community engagement, but the people working on rural electrification truly set the standard for ESB that continues today. They recognised that success depended on the goodwill of farmers and landowners, and the willingness of communities to support us. They had the might of statute behind them, but they looked on that statutory strength as a place of last resort. Their default was to get out, talk and get agreement on what needed to be done. The more connected to the community they were, the better.

They could see the effects that electrification would have on country life, particularly for farming communities, and sold the concept as if they were looking back on the experience. They recognised the influencers within homes and communities and co-opted community groups like the ICA, Macra na Feirme, Muintir na Tíre and of course the local parish priests as advocates. Rural Ireland was still very conservative and resistant to anything too modern, but if the church was in favour, it was generally deemed acceptable!

Women also played a key role in marketing the Scheme, recognising the potential to enhance their own lives. By all accounts, farmers were slow to see beyond the cost until they were asked by young ladies at dances whether they had "got the electricity in?".

It was the ESB rural engineers, the demonstrators and the workers who were the front line in an incredible marketing and sales team. They learned very quickly how to open doors and farm gates even in the most difficult of circumstances. I am sure that the enthusiasm and sense of purpose that the team shared helped to drive its success and overcome the obstacles that they met along the way.

They left a lasting legacy to our organisation, to the rural communities in which they operated and to the development of Irish society. Being part of a large organisation didn't automatically entitle them to respect – they had to earn that respect.

And they did.

It is appropriate that, in celebrating the 70th anniversary of the Rural Electrification scheme, we gather the stories from both our own workers and those on the other side of the fence. This collection ensures many of the tales surrounding one of the most important and transformative projects in the history of the State are recorded for posterity. While the pages of this book may recall a very different time to modern Ireland, they also shine a light into the life of our forebears and we get a sense of the same pride, humour and belonging back then that is still intrinsic in Ireland's people.

Pat O'Doherty,
CEO, ESB

 Energy for generations

1

Sputniks And Brown Bread

Delo Collier

IT was a time when the world was concerned about Sputniks. Those early Russian space satellites were blamed for things that could not be easily explained – a long spell of bad weather, an alteration in the migratory pattern of birds or even the failure of a herring run in a Western fjord. There was a cold war threatened out there, somewhere beyond the horizon. People said prayers for the conversion of Russia, looked to the sky and frowned. Around this time of global concern I was travelling a rutted road in the West of Ireland.

On that day my worries were not related to Kremlin matters, or to the goings-on in Washington, but to the tyres on my car. I had just changed a punctured wheel outside Clifden in Connemara and knew that I had no time to arrange a repair to the damaged tyre. I had an appointment to keep and my heart was anxious, as a recently appointed ESB Demonstrator, that standards would be upheld.

My job was to smooth the transition from solid fuel ranges, cookers and cumbersome domestic arrangements to the new, easy, clean, efficient and labour saving equipment supplied by the Electricity Supply Board. My territory included Connemara, an area of wild beauty but of unforgiving potholes and vicious ruts.

A condition of my appointment was that I should provide my own transport. In reality I neither had a car nor could I drive. My father, himself an ESB employee, took the matter in hand. Without undue fuss he taught me the rudiments of driving and accompanied me when I bought my first car. I was a proud but somewhat nervous first-time motorist on the morning when we collected the car. "Pull in here," he said to me when we came to a wide roadside margin. "I'm off for about half an hour and I want to see one of those wheels changed by the time I get back."

I flustered and protested but he would have none of it. I watched his back as he strolled off down the road and disappeared around a bend. What could I do but take the manual from the glove box?

By the time he returned from his constitutional, I was smeared with oily grease and my knees were bruised from balancing on loose roadside gravel, but the job was done. He tested the wheel nuts, nodded approval and explained that I would be driving the roads of Connemara and would have to change a wheel unassisted. His lesson was well placed. During my time as Demonstrator I replaced so many punctured wheels I could perform the task in my sleep.

On the day I want to tell you about, I was about to be tested to the limits of my calling. I had two calls to make; one concerned a wayward Sputnik, the other concerned brown bread! To add to my worry, I had a punctured wheel sliding about in the boot and I was late for the first appointment. Recalling father's words about changing a puncture while driving in remote places I decided to try to persuade the local garage attendant in Clifden to fix the puncture while I had lunch.

As well as cookers, fridges, washing machines, kettles and irons, the ESB also sold spin dryers. There was a steady demand for clothes dryers in the West of Ireland where sleeveen, unexpected rain could dampen the spirits of any housewife. The vista of rain-sodden sheets forlornly draped along the length of a sagging clothesline and no prospect of a let-up, was enough to drive many to the sherry bottle.

For housewives, the prospect of a spin dryer in the kitchen provided a magical solution to the problem. But there was a snag. The machines that were sold worked well enough. They dried clothes, but the action of high revving dryers on clothes, largely made from natural fibres, could be a little dramatic to say the least. At 3,000 revolutions per minute the spin dryers were inclined to take off and dance around the kitchen. It was a disconcerting sight in an era of new energy. Newspaper articles related stories of satellites in space. These reports were often accompanied by images of revolving contraptions spinning in orbit around the earth. No one was sure how they might be controlled, so why not call those errant spin dryers Sputniks? It seemed appropriate.

I set off, an hour late, for my appointment hoping that my excuse for late arrival would be believed. I steered my little car between ditches of foxglove and fuchsia, careful to ease it over potholes and to avoid stray Connemara blackface sheep, until I noticed the car bumping along a little too much! Yes! You guessed it! Another flat tyre. Nothing for it but to get on with the job of changing the wheel and be glad of the advice given on that day on the roadside when we bought the car! Now quite late for the appointment I pulled up in the yard of the farmhouse near Claddaduff. I could hear the dryer spinning when I knocked at the door. It was a while until the woman of the house appeared. "I turned it on expecting you earlier, Miss Collier. I wanted you to see it leppin' around the floor for yourself. D'you know its like the antics of an auld bachelor farmer at the afters of a wedding. I want to get it to stop dancin' around the kitchen but can't. Sometimes the only way to get it to behave is to sit on it but sure you'd get tired doing that eventually."

She insisted we drink tea and she boiled an egg to go with it as we watched the machine go through the last phases of its dance. When it had gone through its final cycle, I discovered that the floor beneath the machine was uneven and contributing to the erratic behaviour. We found a new location in the kitchen where we could hem it between a dresser and a sideboard. We drank more tea and I forcefully declined another boiled egg while we tested the drier again. This time the performance was greatly improved and the lady seemed much happier with the results. "Himself kept threatening to put a few concrete blocks on it to keep it steady, but I thought that might spoil the look of the place. I'm glad it never came to that."

When I drove out of the yard I had a half-dozen eggs, wrapped individually in pages of the 'Connacht Tribune', to keep me company, but my day was not over yet. There was the matter of brown bread to sort out.

My next call was a half-hour's drive away. A son had emigrated to England to work there on the buildings. A year previously he returned for a summer holiday and he bought his mother a new-fangled electric cooker. The cooker was delivered sometime after his departure back to England. From that time, it sat in the mother's kitchen covered with an oilcloth and was used as a temporary table. Now a year later he was returning once more on vacation and the cooker was still unused. "He always praises my brown bread. I bake for him every day he's home and give him half a dozen loaves to take back with him to the digs. What in God's name will I do if that electric yoke won't bake brown bread?"

As I said, this was a life or death call. Brown bread was the litmus test of a good cook. Many families were reared on the stuff. Now I had to prove to a sceptic that the finished product from an electric oven could match the tried and tested offering from her solid-fuel range. She offered me a cup of tea before I settled into the challenge. She watched me like a hawk as I prepared and mixed and placed the bread into the oven. While we waited for the results she put a boiled egg and a couple slices of her bread before me. I tucked in with a forced enthusiasm. When the moment came to cut and butter my offering, I held my breath. Would this woman's son approve? Was it good enough to export in his suitcase to Kilburn or Cricklewood?

"God," she said, "you'd hardly know the difference."

As I eased myself back towards Galway, the sun was dropping into the Atlantic. I had the window open as I drove. There was turf smoke in the air, autumn was on way, you could smell it. I had a puncture to fix and six free-range eggs to give away.

There's only so many boiled eggs you can face in a lifetime.

Delo Collier, BA, started her career in hospitality management before joining the ESB as a district demonstrator in the Galway area. She managed the ESB Georgian House Museum at 29 Lr. Fitzwilliam and is a volunteer manager with Galway Civic Trust. Delo is also very active in community, archeological and heritage affairs.

2

Love Conquers All

Bridie O'Connor

H E was a plain lad – a big 'Paddy' of a fellow. As a young girl you wouldn't give him a second glance, but he sort of grew on you. That was how I fell for Bill Jones in 1948. I was 19 and working in a grocery and bar in the centre of Mullingar.

This was the bright lights as far as I was concerned. Mullingar was Hollywood excitement compared to the small community town-land I was used to when I was a girl. I was in my element there.

Back then you knew most of the customers who shopped and drank in the establishment, so there was great curiosity regarding the new arrivals, the men putting in the light, the Rural Electrification gang. They'd leave in clothes to be collected for dry-cleaning, buy cigarettes or perhaps have a drink at weekends.

I first noticed Bill Jones the Saturday he came into the shop looking to buy cigarettes. I explained that cigarettes were rationed, as a result of the austerity following the war, and that locals were only allowed 5 per day. Bill explained that he was going to attend a football game in Dublin and pleaded with me to relent. I knew I shouldn't, but he softened something inside me, and I sold him a couple of packets. He offered thanks and promised to bring me back a present from Dublin.

Bill was as good as his promise. When he next came into the shop to drop off laundry he brought me a box of chocolates and an invitation to accompany him to the cinema. I joked that this must be payback for the cigarettes but he insisted that I go, and I finally agreed. He was a tall rugged man and, looking back, you could never call him good-looking, but I saw something beyond that, something much deeper than skin.

Soon I realised that this was the beginning of a lovely romance. He was a perfect gentleman and treated me like a lady. I always felt secure and safe in his company. Bill was over 6ft tall and I was a mere 5ft! He'd call me his 'little angel' or sometimes his 'little lady'. I felt so loved when he was with me.

Sometimes he'd call to the shop just so that he could walk me back to my lodgings in the evenings. It was simple, uncomplicated love.

But the Rural Electrification scheme by its very nature was a moveable one. The roll-out was happening across the countryside. Soon the local work was completed and the gang moved to the next location. We kept in touch and our romance flourished in spite of the obstacles thrown up by distance. Bill arranged taxis to meet me at Ballinasloe railway station so that I could get to my family home some weekends. He moved to work at Ballygar on the Roscommon border and I moved to Galway city to work. This made things easier for us. There was a bus service from Roscommon to Galway that went through Ballygar. Romance was finding ways to overcome obstacles. Amor Vincit Omnia, Love conquers all!

I opened a small shop of my own beside the sea. The future looked promising. Bill had even been to meet my parents a few times. We were going out together for about eighteen months.

But one day two girls came into the shop. They spoke to one another openly in my presence. They said they came from Ballygar and that there were some very nice ESB men working there on the Rural Electrification. One of them boasted about attending a football match with one of them that she fancied. She then said the name of this individual – Bill Jones!

I served the girls politely and pleasantly but it was hard to conceal my devastation. I immediately wrote to him. I challenged his fidelity and told him that I was breaking off our relationship. Bill Jones came to visit me in Galway on the first opportunity that he had. He pleaded with me to relent on my decision. He could not understood what the girls had meant and had not the slightest interest in any girl other than myself. But I held firm and finished our romance there and then. Bill continued to plead with me not to break-up with him, but I did and I now realise that that is one of the greatest regrets of my life.

I am 91 years old and know for certain that I loved Bill Jones and should have believed and trusted him. I was told that he emigrated to America some time soon afterwards.

Rural Electrification may have brightened up the countryside but it left dark spots in two people's hearts that has never been lit.

Almost seventy years later, I hope somehow, somewhere Bill gets to read my memory.

Bridie O'Connor (nee Naughton) is a community volunteer, writer and poet, who lives in the village of Clonberne, Co. Galway.

"When we probed further we found out that she believed the neighbour's family had betrayed United Irishman Michael Dwyer to the Yeoman in 1798."

Alo Brady – 'I Have Lived...'

3

'I Have Lived...'

Alo Brady

THE great Irish wordsmith Patrick Kavanagh was a farmer and then a poet and I think he would have had the perfect eye to record what happened in and around the Rural Electrification scheme.

It might have been sometime earlier when he wrote his Epic poem, but the first few lines – 'I have lived in important places, times when great events were decided' is pure ESB-man language.

All of us who were around from the big roll out in the late forties and down the years could say the same as Kavanagh as we moved about different parts of the country urging people to become part of the great light revolution. We lived in important places – at least for the time of the coming of the light

Like the Inniskeen native, we too found the Iliad in such local rows – and God knows there were plenty of them.

As I press the rewind button on so many incidents and people, I find it invariably stops with the image of Jim Miley, who by any standards was a man apart. He had been with the board from 1926 or '27 and was an outstanding footballer in his day. It was my good fortune to be paired alongside him when he was supervisor in Stratford-on-Slaney in Co Wicklow.

You don't see Jim's kind often nowadays; he was both incredibly competent and caring as a leader of men. And he had a separate vocation in sorting out problems – particularly for women we encountered along the way.

Every Saturday afternoon he would drive his red Beetle home to New Ross and he'd drive back early to begin work on Monday morning. What I liked most about Jim was his compassion.

During our working time together, we must have come across as an unlikely duo – gentleman Jim and me as his sidekick walking into farmyards or drinking in the local pubs. Together though we had a chemistry and between us we did everything from solve rows dating back to Yeomen times to matchmaking as part of our weekly work.

I have lived...

The late John B Keane had nothing on us that time we resided in Wicklow during the Rural Electrification. We stayed in local digs during the week and noticed that the publican, although very handsome, was also a very shy lad. The regulars told us he had been 'walking out' with a girl from Carlow but he was timid in his pursuit of the lady.

Every night we watched this lovely, gentle person as we whetted our thirsts after a long and hard day's work. Finally Jim found out who the lady was that the publican was keen on and informed me that we would be making an excursion across county boundaries the following evening.

This was Jim acting almost as a missionary for the public good. We drove to where the young person lived and he led the chat, leaving her in no doubt that the shy and retiring publican was the one for her.

She had felt slighted that he had not shown any visible interest in their attempts at courtship but Jim guaranteed her that her reluctant suitor actually adored her.

By the strength of his persuasion, they met up and he oversaw their meetings until, like fledglings, he was sure they could fly off together on the wings of love.

I am happy to say that the couple got married and had a very happy life together.

Jim was the proudest man in Ireland the day they tied the knot. And always with a hint of mischief in his voice, he turned to me and said: "Alo, didn't you and me have to drink an awful lot of pints to get that pair up the aisle?"

I have lived...

Jim was about 20 years older than me and had the bearing to defuse even the most traditional of problems. We got word back from the crews that one woman "was not for turning" over allowing poles across her property.

We went to talk to her and found her stubborn as a mule on the issue. "If I get it in, it will mean that crowd of traitors across the way will have access to the light and that will happen over my dead body," she told us.

When we probed further we found out that she believed the neighbour's family had betrayed United Irishman Michael Dwyer to the Yeoman in 1798. She felt it was her duty as an Irish woman never to raise a hand in help to what she perceived as the offending party.

Jim solved the matter in a matter of minutes. "I will assure you here and now that they will never get the power through your poles," he told her.

She believed him and signed up with us to allow the poles across her land. Jim was true to his word. He arranged that the other family got the power in but it came from a different spur.

As we came away that day all we could do was marvel at the woman's loyalty to a rebel's cause which at that stage was over 150 years old. That's what comes flooding back to me from the years out on the road – the strange occurrences, the humour and sense of fun that was attached to even the most tricky of issues we encountered.

And I have to say there were times we had to get out of tight corners of our own making as well.

I have lived...

When we were based around Athy in Co Kildare we used to drink in Jim Nelsen's pub. Jim acted as a local bookie as well, taking bets on matches and the horses or whatever we wanted to wager on. We also drank in Babty Maher's who as well as having the pub, ran an undertaker's business from the same premises.

Now if it was closing time and there were a few still with a thirst on them, we would get the nod and we'd be able to stay on.

However the guards were on the warpath looking for 'found ons' in that period and you had to be resourceful if the loud knock came to your door after hours.

Inevitably we were the subject of such a raid one night. The owner directed us to hide our pints in a coffin before putting a lid on it. He then went and unbolted the front door to let the local sergeant in.

The lawman eyed us suspiciously and asked us why we were still there. The owner told him we were a group who were busily organizing a trip to Lourdes for people of the area – and that was the reason we were in the undertaking part of the premises.

With no sign of drink around and all the patrons wearing their holier than thou faces, he had no choice but to accept the explanation that was proffered.

However it didn't help our cause for further late drinking there when a few nights later, the same sergeant came upon a fella already two sheets to the wind as he was in the process of approaching Babty's front door.

"What do you think you're doing at this hour," enquired the sergeant.

"I was just going to knock," said the inebriated man truthfully.

The sergeant showed a sense of humour in replaying: "Lourdes, the other night, and Knock tonight. This must be the holiest pub in Ireland."

I have lived...

I would need a book on my own to tell you even half of the people I met and the places we got the pleasure of knowing during the rural electrification.

I will endeavour to recall another few incidents and personalities so that they can be recorded in brief form for posterity.

As an Offaly footballer at the time I joined and having just won a county medal with Edenderry in 1951, I had a hand in introducing the legendary Oliver J Flanagan to the family he would marry into some time later.

Around then Oliver J was canvassing on the Monetary Reform ticket and was challenging the status quo in the constituency. It led Canon Burbage in Mountmellick to describe him to the Catholic flock as "the communist in our midst."

He was working as a bricklayer and was doing a line with May McWey. The important figure in that family was Fr Jack McWey – May's brother – who was the chairman of Edenderry GAA club as well as the local priest. Obviously I knew him very well and had a bit of influence with him.

Both of us were based in Laois but Oliver J had a car. The deal was that I got a lift home to training and for my part, I would introduce him to Fr McWey. Once he got on the right side of the reverend gentleman, the man who would be a future government minister never looked back.

I have lived...

I started out in the ESB from Portlaoise in 1950 and was only a short time in the job when there was a 'switch on' in Kilbricken. We had been there working on the project for about nine months before we were ready to bring in the light.

The night before the Phelans, Margaret, Tom and Paddy, hosted a big party in the village in their house.

One man provided a half firkin of Guinness and another for beer to mark the occasion. The Phelans decided to do up the house a bit and Margaret bought a square of linoleum to put down on the stone floor in the kitchen.

The celebrations went on right through the night and by the time the last dancers had left the floor, the lino was worn out. All in one night's dancing! However the Phelans became part of the great ESB clan with Tom becoming a linesman and Paddy a draughtsman in Portlaoise.

I have lived...

I also had the good fortune to work in the west during the roll out of this scheme.

In Bangor Erris, I came across something that I had never encountered before or since – the headless pint of porter.

The locals had traditionally drunk their pint this way because at a time when money was tight, the feeling was that if you had a head of froth on your drink, you had less to consume.

I found trying to drink a pint like that poisonous but the locals in those times would have it no other way.

You met all kinds of people at the time of the rural electrification. Paddy Harte in Sligo told me he was out pegging one day when the farmer asked him if it would be possible to move the pegs three feet towards the ditch.

"Why is that?" asked Paddy.

"Well, if you do, it will act as a stay for a five-bar gate that I want to hang," replied the landowner.

I have lived...

Ted Furey's pub was between Kilcock and Kinnegad on the old road which is now bypassed by the motorway. Back in the 1950s it was a mecca for locals and visitors. Martin Dooley was an ESB man, a real good-looking guy, who was a hit with the ladies. He could also drink for Ireland and among his claims to fame was the fact that he once drank 24 pints of stout in Furey's between last mass on a Sunday and closing time that night.

With so many men having to emigrate to England to find work in that era, the sight of such a handsome man with raven black hair and well over six feet tall drew a lot of favourable comment from the single and some married ladies wherever Martin was located on duty.

Martin also played for the GAA teams which added to the attraction as many tournament games were held at that time which drew huge local crowds.

It led to not just one but several parish priests writing to Mr WP Fox, the ESB's District Manager, informing him that Martin was a danger "to the purity of the ladies" of their parishes and asking if he could be redeployed in some less visible role.

Mr Fox had to be seen to do his duty and summoned Martin in to his office to chastise him. As a lover of the GAA and being of small stature himself, it is true to say that Fox – on seeing Martin in the flesh – ended the meeting full of admiration for the person so complained about.

"Jesus, Sheehan" he said chuckling to his assistant Tom Sheehan, as he watched Martin walk out after their talk. "What a man. For once I think the parish priests have a point."

I have lived...

Finally, I want to tip my hat in memory of a great ESB person who was a true visionary for the company. I can truly say that Paddy (PJ) Dowling was one of the most remarkable men I have ever met. History has already recorded the key role he played in the rural electrification and indeed his overall influence within the organisation.

My recall button however stops away from those heady days and instead focuses in on Paddy as an older man. Fifty years after the first switch on in Oldtown, Paddy was asked to speak at the milestone anniversary of the occasion.

Mindful that he was getting on in age, his son Jim helped him to prepare a speech by having cue cards that he could read off. However once Paddy got to the podium he threw the cards to one side and spoke most eloquently for 20 minutes without once having to refer to a note.

His brain, which had shaped the entire scheme with a few other key people, was as sharp as ever. In fact, Paddy lived around the corner from me in Ailesbury Lawn in south Dublin. His mind was constantly inventing, he could make wheels, he was adept at painting and he made his own gooseberry jam. One day I called up to see him and I got the smell of newly mown grass.

Paddy was over 90 at this stage and I presumed he had either a ride-on or power-driven mower.

"No," he explained. "At my age you need to exercise. That's why I have a push mower. It keeps me in shape."

With a mind and attitude like Paddy Dowling's, it is no wonder that the ESB and indeed the rural electrification became such a groundbreaking journey for the Irish nation. He led from the front with imagination and with a huge appetite to work hard.

It is a legacy that we can fondly hand on to the next generation...

Alo Brady is a former ESB official who edited the company's in-house publication Electrical Mail for over a decade. He was also staff representative on the industrial council. He played football for Offaly and later Sligo and now lives in Dublin.

"We could not feel any more surrounded by nature: far from being lonely, the feeling of being at one with our island, our little space in the universe, was life affirming."

Rhoda Twombly – 'It's 2000 And Power Arrives At Last In Inishlyre

4

It's 2000 And Power Arrives At Last In Inishlyre

Rhoda Twombly

O N September 18, 2000 electricity flowed to Inishlyre, Co Mayo, from the mainland for the first time. Our little island was one of the last places in Ireland to be connected to the mains supply. Such a huge step forward for us but, as is often the case, nostalgia creeps in over time and we tend to forget how awkward life could be without "the electric."

Instead, we remember a gentler time when many chores were timed to the light of the day, the sound of the generator at nightfall a constant background noise and Christmas Day being extra special as it was the only day the gennie (generator) was left on all day. The gennie for the family home was the bane of our Tom's life. A huge yoke encased in a green metal box, the vintage '70s Lister engine could be a bit temperamental, cutting out when it felt like it.

Tom repaired it with zeal: wrenches, screwdrivers and sockets clanging to the concrete floor with increasing vigour as his frustration grew. "You best get out of here, girls – the air's about to turn blue!" he'd say to his sister and me, hovering at the shed door awaiting progress.

When all else failed the only electrician who would touch the anointed gennie would have to be brought in from the mainland for a last-chance repair. Of course, there were many "last chances" for the poor old thing, but she saw us to the arrival of mainland power.

Before then the rule in the house was that the last one up had to go out to the gennie house and switch the beast off. On many cold, black, winter's nights there was the island version of a Mexican stand-off, each of us eye-balling the other to see who would be making a move for bed.

During storms you wouldn't want to be the one to have to go into the black, wet night, torch flashing the way over the beach-side road, prizing open the gennie house door – usually against the wind – to be blasted by the roar of the engine, encased in the smell of diesel.

But on still, idyllic nights – summer or winter – it was a different story. For a moment after switching off, it was as if the world stood still. The silence was dense as it took a minute for ears to adjust to the sudden peace. With the generator put to sleep, it was a pleasure to sit on the bench outside the front gate, senses heightened, to look out on the water and listen to waves gently splashing ashore.

The stars shone, impossibly close and radiant, and we might be treated to an occasional shooting star and a glimpse of the Aurelia Borealis. The smell of diesel was replaced by salt air and sometimes a faint whiff of lobster bait, while bird song cut the dark, the cranes calling to each other from opposite ends of the beach.

We could not feel any more surrounded by nature: far from being lonely, the feeling of being at one with our island, our little space in the universe, was life affirming.

Yes, it was a gentler, slower time. A time of gaslights, candles and conversation around the fire. Of reading by the glow of a double-wicked, pink-globed paraffin lamp, its thin glass chimney so carefully cleaned of soot as it would break if you looked at it wrong. There were even times we were thankful that we didn't have mains electricity, that we had our old generator, when big chunks of the mainland's supply were knocked out by storms.

That's not to say we weren't delighted to hear that plans to electrify Inishlyre were in place in 1999, thanks to Eamon Ó Cuív, the then Minister of State for the Gaeltacht and the Islands, who was determined that the infrastructure of all the populated off-shore islands be improved.

The day the ESB was switched on was life changing; no more trying to do all the chores in the evening while the gennie was on. No more hauling in big, heavy, expensive cans of diesel. No more worrying if the weather would allow us to hang the wash out – although, to this day, the dryer is seldom used. And as cosy and romantic as the rosy-globed double-wick lamp was, reading by its light didn't do the eyes any favours.

Being supplied with mains electricity relatively recently has, in a way, stood us in good stead. The ability to do without power is a skill we retain. The extraordinary ESB repairmen work in dangerous storms to repair the lines that keep us supplied but we are still prepared for the occasional outage.

We keep the wicks of the paraffin lamps trimmed and their reservoirs filled. Torches of all shapes and sizes sit on shelves, bookcases and mantelpieces, and there are plenty of candles ready to light. It can be quite nice occasionally to revisit that quieter, slower time – but a comfort to know we will be returning to the world of light and accustomed convenience fairly quickly.

We hold on to fond memories of island life before we were "switched on," but embrace the advantages we now have. One thing hasn't changed; while the weather on many nights prevents us from sitting on the bench by the sea, calm, idyllic nights will often find us there, reminiscing about the life and times of our little island.

Poet and short-story writer Rhoda Twombly lives on Inishlyre, a small island in Clew Bay with her partner, two dogs, two cats and a small herd of cattle.

"The parson was a very urbane gentleman who was married. As well as attending his flock, he took time out to write on fishing for The Irish Times under the pseudonym of 'Piscator'."

Vincent Fahy – The Power, The Parish Priest And The Protestant 'Piscator'

5

The Power, The Parish Priest And The Protestant 'Piscator'

Vincent Fahy

I GOT to see how people lived in many different parts of Ireland while working with the ESB.

I grew up in Mayo and having qualified as an engineer went working abroad. I came back in 1952 to take up a job in February of that year. I then spent six months in an ESB training school in the company's headquarters where I learned the ropes of what was required to take on a position as a rural engineer.

I dipped my toe in that work as an assistant in Bree between Wexford and New Ross and then moved across to Oylgate where I was in charge.

When I think back now I can only marvel at the gumption of the ESB and Mr Roe and Mr Dowling in particular for giving young engineers like myself our heads. I was always on the move, switching over to Kilmaganny in south Kilkenny, then to Powerstown near Clonmel, after which I went west of the town to Marlfield.

Like a pendulum, I then found myself back the other side in Camolin and Ferns in Wexford before I was transferred up to the Athlone district.

That was slightly unusual at the time as transfers between such districts rarely occurred. Offaly was part of my new responsibility; Carrig between Birr and Borrisokane, then Clareen which was over in Kinnitty direction and then I was based in Kinnitty itself.

You can't but compare the relative wealth of different parts of the country. In Mayo where I grew up, a lot of emigration took place because there was little or no work for the young people.

When I moved to Wexford and Kilkenny you could see how good the land was compared to the small holding in the west and the people were much better off than those I had come across as a child. Offaly was different again. While based there I noticed the chasm between the Protestant and Catholic communities. The Protestants appeared to have better land and had more financial wherewithal as a result.

At the time of my arrival in Kinnitty the difference between the Parish Priest and the Church of Ireland rector could have hardly been more marked. They were polar opposites.

The PP was a blustery type, rough and ready but was obviously influential in the community. His curate was a very engaging man and also very different to his superior.

The parson was a very urbane gentleman who was married. As well as attending his flock, he took time out to write on fishing for the Irish Times under the pseudonym of 'Piscator.'

From the first day I set foot in the place, I was aware of the importance of having the clergy on side. That was easier said than done when the main man was such a domineering character.

I met him virtually every week while the work was going on and to his eternal credit he helped expedite the scheme and smoothed over many problems too.

The women of the area were also in our corner; they'd had enough of the slavery of hauling water in from wells, washing for seven or eight in a bucket or with a washboard.

It was more than just power and light, it was liberation for the rural housewife even above that of their menfolk. It happened for them in stages; the light and the electric kettle were normally the first changes closely followed by the Sacred Heart lamp. Then cookers and washing machines became a factor a bit further down the line.

We were fortunate to have the PP on our side as every time we met, he'd ask me who was in or out. I only referred Catholic families who were not taking the electricity to him. He would then go and talk to them and every time he would get them to change their minds.

As I got to know him better during those weekly communications, he confided in me about problems he himself was having with what he termed "unsavoury characters" in the parish.

One such person was a lady who had a workman living in the same house as herself. The PP felt it was an occasion of public scandal for this to happen and was unrelenting on the issue. He wrote to the Government Minister, Erskine Childers, drawing his attention to the matter but got no reply.

He took great umbrage at this slight and soon after when he heard the Taoiseach of the day Eamon De Valera was planning to visit the area, he let him know in no uncertain terms that he wasn't welcome.

When you are working, it is often wise to have lodgings outside of the area. I stayed in a hotel in Birr, which was owned by a great rugby man in the town. I played outhalf and enjoyed the experience of being able to play a game away from the soap operas that surrounded the installation of electricity at that time.

That's not to say that even the rugby was free of rancour. Mr Egan was known to show his displeasure with some of our team by coming in off the sideline and whacking players who weren't performing to his liking with a stick that was forever in his company.

There were big characters around the place for sure but none quite as formidable as the PP. However, I met him one day when he was crestfallen and so totally nonplussed with life that he was barely able to speak.

I asked him what was wrong.

"My work is totally stymied," he told me. "That woman (referring to the lady with the workman living in her house) came to see me yesterday.

"She asked me bluntly- 'What is your problem with me?' I told her it was a scandal to have a workman living under the same roof.

"And do you know what she said to me? 'Isn't your housekeeper living under the same roof as you and is that not a bigger scandal?'"

He clearly struggled that people might think like this and also that the woman stood up to him on the issue.

However much that incident rumbled around in his head, it was nothing compared to his state of mind in the run-up to the switching on ceremony. Now this was always a really big occasion and everyone looked forward to it.

At the beginning of the scheme in the area he had insisted that

Catholics should get the electricity in first. We smoothed over that without ever complying with his wishes. Now as the big switch on approached, he went into overdrive by saying that the other side's reverend gentleman couldn't be up on the rostrum with all the dignitaries.

Furthermore he insisted that Tom F O'Higgins should not be invited nor would Oliver J Flanagan who represented the area. His reason for wanting Oliver J off the guest list he told me was because he was in the village some time before, on the night of the Corpus Christi procession. His objection was that the public representative had used the altar where the PP previously had the Blessed Sacrament exposed to his congregation, to address a rally.

"He's definitely not coming," he repeated.

Although the other reverend gentleman would have represented a large percentage of the community at the time, the PP had his own ideas of who should be on the stage.

I went to see how the pastor felt about it. He found it all quite amusing and said he had no problem about not being among the dignitaries.

He explained that he would obviously have to go but would keep a low profile and allow the PP a free run.

On the night, he was content to take his place in the crowd though he was promoted to the front row on the floor.

Oliver J wasn't there but Mr O'Higgins was part of the main party on stage with the Parish Priest and the local headmaster among others.

He wasn't over enamoured when he gazed around the hall and spotted his opposite number in the front row. Before he was called on to bless the switch, he went out to the front of the stage to shake Holy Water down on the crowd. He particularly laced a fair shower of it on top of the leader of what he called "the disaffected brethren."

The rural electrification taught us how to meet challenges like this and negotiate our way around them. It was the same out there with the work to get poles through land without farmers and other such stakeholders causing delays.

After leaving the midlands, I headed to north Donegal before returning to north Mayo where I was made a group engineer based in Ballina.

One of my first jobs was to extend the electricity to Belmullet from Crossmolina through Bangor Erris. It was all bog and very challenging from an engineering point of view to get proper foundations for poles. I also had to be mindful that cost was an important factor, so we had to do the work as cheaply as possible without cutting corners.

In Belmullet, Martin McIntyre had a licence to provide electricity with a diesel engine. He supplied about one third of the population with a few poles in the street. We had no choice but to buy his rights out and I can tell you he did very well out of it.

He gave me a large calendar from Pan Am Airlines after the switch on. It was big and glossy and I kept it for ages afterwards. He was decent man and a significant figure in the development of the Erris peninsula.

He made a lot of his money bringing sods of turf to Dublin in fleets of yellow trucks. He was a true entrepreneur.

Unfortunately, there wasn't enough of his ilk in Mayo to prevent the massive emigration from around there to England and America.

I was raised in that area of the country and was lucky that my parents had a shop. Most of the others came from land which in reality was bad bog. Often the children didn't have sufficient clothes to wear while shoes were a luxury they didn't even consider.

There was only one real choice for those youngsters when they became adults and that was to go away and hope for a better life.

I had great regard for the nuns in Foxford who opened their charity woollen mills to give people the prospect of work.

A Sister from the O'Mahony family from Cork couldn't believe the abject poverty people were suffering when she first arrived in the area. It appears she had innate entrepreneurial skills as she saw that the River Moy had a fall on it, providing the opportunity to generate power.

She then collected money from her own religious order and set up the woollen mills which at one time employed up to 200 people.

I will end by returning to Offaly for a story that appears more apocryphal than true but did in fact happen.

One of the rural engineers was seen as something of a soft touch when dealing with landowners. Often he would agree to move poles into ditch areas rather than having them traversing and ruining their fields.

His direct boss, Paddy Fox, heard about this and was unhappy that one of his men was caving-in to locals.

No one knew the workings of the ESB better than Fox. If he complained and tried to get this man removed from his district, he knew he would have him in his team for life.

Instead Fox took advantage of a day up in Dublin to talk to the big wigs in the organisation and at every turn he extolled the virtues of the engineer. He reminded them that he had been in Germany with Siemens, could speak the language and implied they were missing out by not having his talent as a resource for Head Quarters' business.

The man duly was promoted to Dublin but they soon saw they had been out-Foxed and tried to move him out.

Revenge for the slighted engineer was served up in the Gaiety Theatre where his play about the organisation contained names and characters that were easily identifiable.

Best of all from his point of view was that he was the central character in the play and was able to even the score with many of his adversaries from such a vantage point.

Vincent Fahy (88) began as a rural area engineer in the ESB and held several senior positions around the country and in Boston. Following a stellar career in the organisation, he retired in 1990.

6

The Wonders Of The Electric Fence

Pauline Brew

IT was the 1950s and our farm in north Cork had just been connected to electricity. Everyone was mesmerised by the fact that at the flick of a switch the big farmhouse kitchen was bathed in light. No more Tilley lamps to be lit even if they were quite nice to look at.

The women talked about the gadgets they might get when the creamery cheque came in. They had heard you could buy electric irons, washing machines of all things, and even electric cookers. They dreamed about all the free time they would have with all these labour-saving devices doing all the work.

All they had known up to then was the drudgery of the daily tasks. Washing the clothes for a large family took most of one day. Usually Mondays. The water was drawn from the well and boiled in big saucepans on the range. Using sunlight soap and a washing board the clothes were scrubbed and put through a mangle to squeeze the water out of them. They were then hung outside in summer. In winter they were hung over the range. It was hard to imagine that there was a machine that could do all this.

The men had other concerns. My father was one of the first in the area to buy an electric fence. He erected it around the front field to keep the cows from straying into the next field. The fence delivered a shock that was enough to frighten off the cattle but not enough to do any lasting harm. However, my brothers and sisters and I had a different plan for the fence altogether.

We had a problem of our own. Every year without fail we had a visit from our cousin in England. His parents and ours thought that it would be good for him to spend a few weeks on the farm. They also thought it would be educational for him to see how a farm worked; and to spend time with his cousins. In those days nobody consulted the children as to how they felt. It was made plain to us that it was our job to entertain him.

He spoke with a really posh accent and was properly dressed. Our parents doted on him and treated him like very delicate china. We were resentful as he got the first slice of cake, the nice crunchy crust of the newly baked bread and the cream from the top of the milk. He was a little older than us and was also allowed to stay up later. We all had our jobs to do but he was never asked to do a hand's turn. We were really mad at the unfairness of it all.

We tried to discourage him from coming. We had taken him down the fields and often managed to lose him but he still arrived back safe and sound. We brought him out to the stream that bordered our land and he had ended up falling in the water. We had given him a bumpy ride on the hay cart in the hope of offending his constitution. We even locked him in the shed. None of these measures worked.

The electric fence was the last card we had to play.

We plotted and planned. We had all got shocks from the electric fence but we were used to it. It gave you a tingle up your arm. You could hear it ticking and we soon learned that if you counted the ticks you could catch it and not get a shock. It was all a matter of timing. Of course, we didn't tell him any of that.

After tea one evening we suggested playing out in front of the house before we edged over in the direction of the fence. We all gripped it in turn counting the ticks in our heads. Watching us, he gripped it with both hands. We waited with baited breaths. Next thing he screamed and did a vertical take off high into the air. His face turned white with the sheer fright.

Eventually he ran towards the house calling out for my mother. It took her a long time to calm him down with milk and biscuits. He was mollycoddled for the rest of the evening. We thought that was a bit of a sickener as he lapped up all the attention. We also wondered why he was making such a drama out of it all.

Despite this, we remained reasonably friendly to him for the remainder of his stay. In truth, we probably felt a little ashamed of ourselves... but only a little.

The following summer a letter arrived from England saying he wouldn't be gracing us with his presence that year. My mother often wondered why. My brothers and sisters never answered her musings but were thankful that the rural electrification had come in time to save our summers from then on.

Pauline Brew grew up near Charleville, Co Cork but is now a resident of Co Limerick. She is married with three grown-up children and four grandchildren and writes as a hobby.

"Yet, on a lovely sunny morning in the month of May when I rode my bike the six miles to the rural office all those years ago, it was like winning the lotto."

**Michael Lynch –
From Lights To Light Moments**

7

From Lights To Light Moments

Michael Lynch

IT was a day in school in the year of 1948 and the master was reading the daily paper when he turned to the class and asked if anyone know the meaning of the words 'rural electrification.' He also asked if we could spell 'electrification.'

For the record, one boy knew both. Little did I know that day how the Rural Electrification Scheme would shape my later life for 46 years.

The ESB had a large number of crews working all over Ireland at that time. The crews would consist of 20-30 workmen, foreman, linesman, one or two drivers, one engineer and one supervisor.

They'd rent a premises in the area for a few months as an office and a store. Thirty to 40 local men were hired for the few months to dig the holes by hand and pull out the conductor.

In the mid-fifties the wages were five pound, six shillings per week. The foremen and linesmen got about two pound more. That was for a 49-hour week which included a half-day Saturday. The permanent staff got protective clothing that consisted of a long brown waterproof coat and one pair of wellingtons each year.

Yet, on a lovely sunny morning in the month of May when I rode my bike the six miles to the rural office all those years ago, it was like winning the lotto. To get a job with the ESB at that weekly rate was a big improvement on the £2 a week I was earning with a local blacksmith. There were about 40 men outside the office looking for work when I arrived, and about half of them got started.

I think the reason I got the job was because the schoolmaster had already submitted my name. We put our bikes up on the lorry and were dropped off at work sites around the area. When it came to my turn, I was told to take my pick, shovel and crowbar up a laneway where I would meet a foreman.

I met a big tough-looking man who just about spoke to me. We climbed up to the top of a hill where we found a wooden peg in the ground. He said: "Six feet, six inches and be finished as quick as you can."

I lost some sweat digging that first hole for the ESB in the blazing sun, in ground as hard as metal. I was lucky though; that same tough man took me under his wing, brought me with him and shaped my destiny within the company.

The main rural scheme ran from 1946 to around 1961; large pockets of the country weren't completed until much later because they were too remote while others resisted for years before finally welcoming in the light.

The ESB introduced a Post Development Scheme that lasted for years where people had to make a contribution to get the light. This work was mostly carried out by the permanent ESB depots in the big towns.

Some rare characters started to work in the rural electrification scheme. Most were farm labourers who never had a set time to start or finish work. Some struggled to dig a hole a day and were so afraid they'd be sacked that they continued working after six o'clock for nothing to get the job done.

There was no 10 o'clock break which meant workers had tea once a day. We had no way of making tea except for an old black kettle the gang brought to the nearest house to ask the lady to boil it for them.

Everyone had his own little packet of tea which was poured into the big kettle. Often the woman of the house would bring out a mug of tea if a crew was working beside her but that was very much at her discretion.

I saw a man one day digging a hole and noticed he only had one sleeve on his shirt. I asked what happened and he explained that the head was loose on the pick. He had nothing to tighten it with so he tore the sleeve off to tighten the head.

Another time we were pulling a conductor across a field of

carrots. It was a Saturday and the foreman was leaving for home on a half-day to his wife and family. This particular man was always looking to have something extra to take with him. The carrots caught his eye but even though he searched high up and low down, he couldn't find a bag to put them in.

He went behind a hedge, took off his long johns and knotted the bottom of each leg. With his makeshift knapsack of carrots on his back, he headed out on the road to thumb a lift home happy as Larry.

Everyone has an unforgettable moment from the Rural Electrification and it often is a tale against themselves. Mine certainly was.

One day passing a house I saw a wee woman standing in the doorway. I asked her for a drink of water and she said: "Surely gauson, but would you rather a mug of buttermilk?"

She rushed across to a shed with a half-door and came back with a mug full to the brim. I drank it all and it was lovely. "Well," she said, "if you want more, there is a big tub of buttermilk on the floor in the shed."

The only problem was that there were also three big red hens sitting on the edge of the tub with their tails facing into the buttermilk... I'm sure I got a lot more than I bargained for.

As crews moved to new areas, they soon sussed out both the quality of digs ... and the local talent.

We had one womaniser in the group who seemed to be always in the right place at the right time.

On one occasion he got digs with this lady who lived on her own. Every day he came into work with big bags of sandwiches, a smile on his face and with the proud boast that she was feeding him like a horse.

A short while later another ESB man was putting up a meter board in this lady's house. One of the lads asked what the place was like. He said it was very well kept but he found evidence to suggest our colleague was sleeping with the landlady.

"How do you know that?" we asked. "Well," he said, "the bedroom door was open and I think I seen two pos under the bed."

His job was to instal meter boards and in another place he came to this house where – you've guessed it – another lady was living alone.

He told her: "I think the best place to instal your meter is in the bedroom because the ceiling is higher." She readily agreed but some days later when the electrician arrived he couldn't believe his eyes when he saw the meter board in the bedroom.

He reported it to his supervisor who in turn gave our womaniser a right dressing down for doing such a thing.

"Well," said the man in his defence, "the woman didn't mind a bit and if you talk to her you will find the ESB has another satisfied customer in this area."

Michael Lynch is a former long-standing ESB official from Co Cavan. He is married with eight grown-up children and enjoys writing as a hobby

8

Before The Light
Joe Kearney

MY grandfather had a distrust of the world. He was stubborn and self-sufficient. At the time I remember him he was an old man on crutches. He'd tell you that he lost the use of his legs standing in a cold river tickling salmon. Obstinacy should have been his middle name, but I will always be grateful to him for his mulishness, because if my grandfather had not been so dogmatic, I might never have known a time before the light.

In the early decades of the fledgling state, our district of Kilkenny was included in the grand plan that was Rural Electrification, 'or getting in the light' as it was known locally. Neighbour after neighbour signed up for the brown wall-switches and the Chinese-hat shades and the meter boxes.

The tall poles approached from all sides but my grandfather dug in and refused to subscribe to electrical progress. The argument he presented to my distracted grandmother, or to anyone else who would listen, was that if every house in Ireland was connected to one power source by means of wires and cables, then all some madman had to do was drop one bomb on Shannon and, to quote himself: "We'll all be blown up in our own beds."

As the poles delivering the currency of new enlightenment advanced across the landscape they reluctantly veered away from my grandfather's house, unable to overcome his stout resistance.

New light shone out from bulbs and poked nosey brightness into previously darkened corners of our neighbours' lives. It somehow seemed to make them shy of one another as if they had been rendered naked publicly and cobwebby secrets dragged into the open.

The new brightness could be sharp and harsh. It took getting used to. The softly cloaking shadows had vanished except for those remaining on in my grandfather's house.

He was comfortably at ease with the waxy smell of paraffin, the guttering glow of candles and the soft-focus of firelight. The old man found the sources of this gentle lighting conducive to contemplation, to summoning up old ghosts and past events. The sigh of collapsing embers was the echoed exhalation of his own memories when he rewound the spool of recollection while safely embraced in the folds of his armchair.

The flickering shadow play on the uneven bruising of the old walls kindled his imagination every bit as much as the wall paintings at the caves in Lascaux, France had done for prehistoric man. The smoke from lamps and candles was the cloud he needed through which he'd filter his musings into patterns that suited him. It was preferable to him to remember people and places of his past not as bright and sharp but wavering and blurred around the edges.

There were panes of glass in his windows that also provided him with this comfort. Some were imperfect prisms composed of a material known as 'war glass'. It gave the viewer a distorted image of the world. It comforted my grandfather in some way just knowing that there was not a need for perfection. Plato was correct; what we mortals looked upon was a mere imitation of reality.

When he finally surrendered up his philosophical cogitation and his fireside chair and left this place of mortal flaws for a more divine environment, it was my grandmother who welcomed the light into our lives. We were reeled-in in one final round up of ditherers, stragglers and backsliders.

When they came to instal the light, I marvelled at the tall pole that stood outside our ditch. I observed the stalactites of blackened pitch that ran down and hardened along the length of its surface like drips of grease on a giant candle. It resembled the mast of a voyaging vessel, its unfurled sails fastened by silver hawsers of wire rope. I pressed my face against it to smell the exotic strangeness. "Come away from there child. You'll be killed," my grandmother screamed at me, perhaps remembering the old man's dire warnings.

There would be no return from that moment onwards. Snakes of dark wires trailed across our walls and ceilings like coils of liquorice tails; the switch as thrown and the darkness banished for good. No more trimming of wicks or removing candle-wax, instead my grandmother swept and dusted newly illuminated corners, disposed of cobwebs and ousted colonies of long-established spiders.

In all respects, my grandfather's prophecy was wrong. The wires coming into our homes didn't cause our destruction. But who knows, perhaps he foresaw that by banishing one set of cobwebs we would replace them with another form of 'web', this one even more ensnaring than what had gone before?

That blinded by artificial light we would no longer see the stars, become lost and lose our fix on the world. And surely that is as equally frightening as being "all blown up in our own beds."

Joe Kearney is a writer, broadcaster and award-winning documentary maker.

"Sunlight never travelled further than the front doorstep. How that golden blade of sunlight teased and tantalised as it crept up the step. Our children tried to cup it in their hands and bring it indoors."

**Eileen Casey –
Black Night To Sacred Light**

9

From Black Night To Sacred Light

Eileen Casey

C HILDREN of the 1950s will have many personal memories associated with the installing of electricity. In my case, however, our house was already illuminated when I was born, the youngest of six children as it happens.

Wires were tacked over the wallpaper, or ran across the ceiling with no thought for aesthetics. All we cared about was being able to tune into Radio Luxembourg, watch RTE and be able to read in bed – a real luxury on a winter's night.

Of course, I'd often wondered what the house was like before we became 'electrified,' hearing tales of studying by an oil lamp's light, pillar candles and cooking by either gas or Stanley range.

It took my husband, John, to tell me what those pre-light days were really about and how he interpreted light and shade as he grew up on the Muckross Estate in Killarney, County Kerry.

He remembers going with his father to fish by the lake under the shelter of Torc Mountain. When the season landed, they'd set off at dusk. There was just enough natural light to get them through the woods onto the lakeshore.

While by the lake, night descended quickly and moonlight flickered over the silvery waters. Plentiful flies meant that trout fattened and drew nearer to the surface to reap the bountiful supply.

Father and son worked by instinct and senses. Ears were finely tuned for the sudden splash or ripple of water. Oftentimes, campfires on the shore threw up a blaze of colour and it must have seemed so simple and close to nature, the world of father and son.

Coming back through the woods with the newly caught fish was like stepping into black and being enveloped in it. They'd turn on the torches then but if the battery was low, John would feel a leap of fright in his chest which was (nearly) always reassured by the grip of his father's hand.

They'd hear the crackle of twigs underfoot or the skittering of animals among the oaks, ash and willow trees which grew in abundance around the row of cottages where they lived side-by-side with neighbours who made up a real community.

When our own children were small, we spent many happy summers in that tree-lined place. The cottages were set so far back from the road and because they were surrounded by trees and faced into Torc Mountain, sunlight never travelled further than the front doorstep. How that golden blade of sunlight teased and tantalised as it crept up the step. Our children tried to cup it in their hands and bring it indoors.

Sometimes they pretended they had captured it and they'd place it in the middle of the floor as if it were a precious spark of summer that would suddenly flow into every nook and cranny of that house.

At least we could switch on the light but back in the early fifties, that kitchen must have been like a coalmine in the Welsh valleys. John was eight or nine years old when the transformation came. Instead of a kitchen lit only by small halos of light (from embers of cigarettes, firelight or candles), a new dawn was literally born.

The ESB men installed the fuse-box over the door and put in sockets upstairs and down. Again, there was little thought for aesthetics. No one could afford the hassle of tearing down and repapering walls. Plaster usually came away with each stripping and insulation was unheard of at the time. Getting in the 'electric' meant that a television could be bought – in his case a gift from an American aunt. Cooking was still done on gas and it was always a great back-up in case a storm might hit and knock out the whole shebang.

Which was what happened in 1961 when Hurricane Debbie decided to wreak destruction. A branch of a big oak tree fell on the transformer pole and plunged the row of cottages into darkness. Debbie originated from a tropical disturbance over Central Africa...a fact that meant very little to the folk who lived near Torc Mountain.

This tropical 'hussy' intensified to Category 3, passing over Ireland, bringing record winds of 114mph. Tens of thousands of trees and power lines were knocked but there were few telephones 'in them days'. The men who lived in the cottages tried lifting the tree off the transformer pole, causing a great whoosh which could have signalled their end. They then left well enough alone and waited for the ESB men to come out and restore their home comforts.

So I never experienced the 'joys' of oil lamps and candles or cooking salted mushrooms on a hot range. I remember, however, that there was a house in my midlands street still without electricity long after everyone else had been hooked up.

Sarah was the woman's name, a 'character' if ever there was one. She lived on her own and was quite happy with things as they were. Sarah rose early and went to bed early and had no time for television. She had an old battery radio and if the humour was on her she'd listen to it. Entering her house as a child with a message was like going into a cavern. I had to readjust my vision to accommodate the semi-darkness and the shadowy shapes of Sarah's north facing kitchen.

What persuaded her in the end to get the elctricity in was the Sacred Heart lamp. Sarah wanted that red glow so badly that she finally succumbed to the inevitable.

It was her proudest moment when the Sacred Heart throbbed its fiery response after she had it plugged in above the radio.

Eileen Casey is an established writer who spends her time between South Dublin and the Midlands.

"She was known to sell the tricoloured Neapolitan from time-to-time and maybe some Raspberry Ripple if someone was home from England, but Banana flavour was never a big hit in Redhills."

**Joe Brady –
Trouble Coming From On High**

10

Trouble Coming From On High

Joe Brady

MY mother had a shop in Redhills, County Cavan near the border. The grocery was located on a crossroads in the town, a great place for people to congregate; for men to play pitch-and-toss and for young lads like myself to trick-act on bicycles.

Whenever Duffys or Fossetts or Chipperfields circus visited we would be full of high-wire antics for weeks. Each one of us had notions of the acrobats we might become if only given half a chance. When we saw the lads coming around with the Rural Electrification, we were fascinated.

Gravity ensured that we walked with our feet firmly rooted to terra firma, however these men could walk up poles without any apparent effort. Our mouths hung open when we saw what they could do. This was circus stuff performed by mortals. If they could do it...well then so might we!

Around this time we subscribed for the electricity. My mother thought that selling ice cream might be a boost to the shop, so we bought a 'fridge. She hung a flapping plastic sign, supplied by the dairy, outside the front door and before long they came flocking in for wafers.

This was before the time that ice-cream sellers began using a plastic measuring gauge to determine the size of a thruppeny, sixpenny, or God preserve us, a penny wafer. All she used was her eye to set the dimensions of each sale. Now, you have to consider who she was selling to. There were bachelor farmers coming to her after Sunday Mass for a sixpenny wafer who could gauge the health, weight and value of a beast by just casting a sideways glance as they were cycling past a distant field. If there was a millimetre wanting in her offering, then these men would know. She walked that narrow line between success and failure when it came to ice cream sales and she knew the dangers.

There was a high demand for Vanilla in those heady days of that first summer. She was known to sell the tricoloured Neapolitan from time-to-time and maybe some Raspberry Ripple if someone was home from England, but Banana flavour was never a big hit in Redhills.

I recall the Sunday that I was playing with a Yo-Yo outside the shop door when one particular customer strolled out into the sunshine. He had a particularly thick sixpenny in his fist and looked mightily pleased with the purchase.

I now realise why the wafer was so generously cut – my mother had run out of Vanilla. He nodded absently to me before taking a lick from the wafer that would have done justice to a suck calf. I watched as he wrinkled up his face and threw the ice cream over the hedge with a vengeance. He looked at me as if the entire experience was my fault. "Well blast that woman and her ice-cream, she must have p****d on the bloody thing."

Poles seemed to sprout up overnight in fields where they looked strange as fallen moonstone. One late afternoon I wandered homewards with a school pal. We were talking about the wireman and the pole walking. We saw where they had finished work for the day; saw a newly erected pole and went over to investigate. You could smell the fresh creosote and the soil was newly tramped down all around the base.

That was when my pal saw the irons, the boots the men used to climb the poles. They were bright yellow in colour and thrown in under a furze bush with a collection of shovels, pick axes and a crow bar. The iron boots had straps to hold your foot and spikes on the toes to grip the timber as well as a crescent hoop at the front that went around the circumference of the pole.

I was uncertain, but my school-pal could not be discouraged, he put on the irons and went over to climb the pole. "There's no one about to stop us," he said, "and who will ever know?"

He commenced the climb and all went well until he was about halfway up. I could see him starting to tire and wobble. His feet were strapped into the boots but they kept slipping. The one thing we failed to understand when we observed the wiremen was that in addition to the iron boots, they also wore a leather belt that they strapped about the pole and moved with them as they climbed.

It kept them upright. As with the circus, there's a trick to everything. I heard the scream as he fell backwards. He broke both his ankles, suspended upside down from the pole.

It is a sound that I will never forget.

I ran for help and he was eventually taken down to the ground. The one thing, we could not understand, was why despite his considerable pain he kept insisting that the climbing irons be removed from his feet.

Afterwards, when I visited him in hospital, he explained: "I thought I was in enough trouble climbing the pole without anyone having to know that I'd stolen the boots as well."

The world was a simpler place back then, even if we had no appetite for Banana flavoured ice cream!

Joe Brady is a car enthusiast, community volunteer and a Cavan man, who although living in Dublin, never really left home.

"Now as anyone who ever worked on a farm knows, there is nothing better to gladden the heart of a farmer than to a see a potential loss turn into a tangible gain."

**John Fitzpatrick –
Lights, Sales, Action**

11

Lights, Sales, Action

John Fitzpatrick

MANY of us working for the ESB were on a mission to sell the idea that electricity would be a good thing to have in a house or on a farm.

At the time plenty of people were progressive and couldn't wait to have it installed but there were others who refused point blank to have anything to do with us.

My job was to change their minds so that we could get the poles across their land and onto the next house.

I have three great memories of my time where I was successful simply by using different selling techniques.

The first case involved a big farmer around Moneygall who had a huge number of cows. His son approached me on the quiet to see if I could persuade his father to get the power in as it took hours to hand-milk the herd.

He was a very abrupt sort of man and no matter what way I approached the subject, he had a quick way of shutting the door on any further conversation.

I decided that the best thing to do was to meet fire with fire.

"It's a pity we don't encounter more people like you," I said to him, immediately grabbing his attention at my change of tactic.

"Sure this thing is costing the ESB a packet and all you have to do is allow poles in and pay for a plug and a socket. I tell you sir, if I came across more of your type, I would make fierce saving altogether for the company."

That was the last thing the man wanted to hear and when it dawned on him that it was the ESB or the government that was paying out the big money on this, he couldn't wait to have it installed. The wink from the son as I left the farmyard told me I had handled a contrary man very well.

Another time I was passing the field of a man who refused to let the poles go across his land near Monasterevin in Co Kildare. I was dressed up smartly in suit, shirt and tie and heard a commotion from near the roadside ditch.

On further perusal I could see that a heifer was having difficulty calving. The man was running around shouting and his son was standing near the distressed animal.

Seeing my opportunity, I shouted in: "Can I be of any help, lads."

The instant reply from the father was; "Not unless you're a vet."

Initially I had thought the son might be a vet, but seeing as neither were great in this situation and I had pulled several calves on our own farm, I jumped across the gate and went up to them.

Discarding the coat of my suit and rolling up the sleeves of my clean shirt, I could see the farmer looking at me with great curiosity. "Give us a hand so," was all he said as he watched me getting ready to go to work.

I inspected the heifer and when I put my hand in I could feel that the calf's head was too far down for her to give birth naturally.

It took a bit of time but I managed to get my hand down underneath the head and pushed it up into her birth passage way. I'd say I was up to 15 minute manoeuvring before I caught the two legs and pulled down, allowing the calf to slide out gently onto the ground.

Now as anyone who ever worked on a farm knows, there is nothing better to gladden the heart of a farmer than to a see a potential loss turn into a tangible gain.

Instead of having to call a vet and pay a king's ransom to save mother and bull calf, this stranger had walked in from the road, dirtied his good clothes and presented him with a healthy addition to his herd.

The man couldn't thank me enough and asked me where I was from. I told him I was with the ESB and there and then he promised me that anything I ever wanted from him could be considered a done deal.

We had the poles lined up across his land within days and he couldn't do enough to help us.

It was back in Moneygall in south Offaly that I encountered the most surreal experience of my time selling the light to the public. This was a case where two old ladies not only refused to have poles across their land but also objected to people interfering with their property.

They had a history with neighbours who had tried to carry out drainage work but to no avail. The word was to stay away from those old ladies.

When I heard this, it made me all the more determined to see if I could win them over. I still remember the day I walked up their avenue and the feeling of being involved in a Hitchcock-type film as the trees cast a long shadow over the old house.

In the gathering gloom of the evening, I knocked on the door and waited apprehensively as I could hear the shuffle of feet from the other side.

When the door opened, I was taken aback to see an elderly woman with a goitre the size of a melon on her neck staring up at me.

She certainly was frightening to look at though I must have hidden my shock as I introduced myself with a smile and asked if I could have a few minutes of her time.

Instead of the resistance that I was promised would meet me, she invited me inside where an open fire was the only means of lighting in the living room.

Immediately my senses were attacked by the pervasive smell of cats' pee. I tried to hide my reaction again as she introduced me to her sister. They invited me to have tea. It was the last thing I wanted in those surroundings but I knew I had to say 'yes' if I was to get into their good books.

We chatted about various things as we sipped our tea and then one of them flummoxed me by asking if I expected to see my loved one again in the next world.

I said I had no doubt I would if they were in the right place. They seemed to like my answer and we continued to talk about family and times past.

Then one of the ladies said if I would become their 'daddy' for the day by overseeing what should happen, they would allow the electricity across their lands. This was music to my ears. As for taking responsibility for the work on their land I told them that nothing would give me greater pleasure.

And so it came to pass that they signed up and I hope they have indeed met their real daddy and other loved ones after they passed on.

I got nothing only good luck from my time in Moneygall. Tea in every house and a bride of 55 summers. Josie Ryan was actually doing a strong line when I first encountered her thanks to an introduction by my dear departed friend, Tim Liffey. Eleven children followed and my time on the Rural Electrification brought me only luck and happiness.

I played hurling for Laois as a corner back for many years but the only All Irelands I won were with the ESB. The company started an inter-district GAA tournament in hurling and with fellows in our area coming from Kilkenny, Tipperary, Laois, Offaly and Carlow, it was no surprise we were All Ireland champions nearly every year.

John Fitzpatrick (81) is a former ESB employee who played hurling for Laois. He is married to Josie and they have 11 children.

12

Another Way To Skin The Cat

Denis O'Higgins

I T was the black and white days of the late fifties, when rural time moved at snail pace and nothing changed or improved, merely rotated from one season to the next.

Each new month dictated the mundane manual work programme on the cluster of small uneconomic farms in our locality. Now and then the talk was of the new energy source called electricity that was sweeping across parts of Ireland, areas that we and our neighbours had only heard of, and weren't sure if such places existed at all.

Some argued that the electricity would be carried on poles placed along the public road and would be very dangerous. Wiser voices who had travelled far confirmed that the ESB poles would be erected on farmland to carry the new power from one dwelling to the next.

Most householders in our locality were opposed or indifferent to this scheme as they didn't value the need for it or its intrusion into their lives. There was also a fear of the unknown but the greatest drawback was that it would create a bill that few could afford.

The local debate was quietened by the arrival of the gangs of robust men who walked through the fields with their maps and markers. They rarely bothered to establish the name of the landowner or ask permission before entering or operating on private property.

It was different times and the ESB personnel would have known that despite mutterings of local disapproval, the affected farm owners would not dare question any actions from an official body.

One thing that caused great concern was the positioning of the poles. Some could have been positioned beside a fence or a natural boundary but were instead placed some distance out, thereby spoiling the field.

It was on a Friday evening when the ESB ganger hammered a hazel stick into the hallowed soil of our front lawn. This marker was the usual signal indicating to the gang where the next pole should be erected.

My mother was furious as, if erected the way the ESB wanted, it would spoil her precious lawn. Worse than that, the pole and its wires would spoil for ever the view of and from our house.

Her first thought was to talk to the ganger and appeal to his 'better nature' but the word back was that this official didn't have a 'better nature.' He was a man of few words, who laid down his law in rigid terms.

Instead of asking him to choose an alternative site and so draw attention to our plight, we ignored him altogether. After all we had until the following Monday to frustrate his plan. There was always another way of skinning that cat and we had to find the means.

From early the following Saturday morning all siblings, small and big, were assembled and prepared for hours of hard manual work. My mother decided that a flower and shrub bed would be created in the corner of our small lawn, where a "threatening" hazel stick now resided. The first thing to do was find a new home for the wooden imposter. The hazel was exiled and hammered into place some 15 yards away, in an adjacent field. She took great care to ensure it was kept in line with the poles already erected on either side.

We worked like never before carrying suitable stones until a two-foot high semi-circle wall enclosed the corner of our lawn. The next task was to carry buckets of soil and manure until the selected area slowly filled up to the wall level. Lastly we transplanted flowers and a few gawky shrubs onto our new bed. My mother did a few final adjustments so that her new arrival got a more mature appearance, all for the purpose of subterfuge and camouflage.

As always the ESB crew arrived early on the Monday with all their equipment for the day's work laid out in our front area. I spied on them through a window with a mixture of excitement and fear of what would follow.

The group of four shuffled and foostered about for some minutes scratching their heads. Instinctively, they felt something was amiss but failed to solve the puzzle. Fortunately, they began the normal digging at the spot we had relocated them to by moving their marker.

Within a short time the new pole was raised and put permanently into place.

When the ganger arrived on his routine inspection late that afternoon, I watched again through the window as he muttered to himself. He took stock, looked at angles and began shaking his head. He knew what had happened.

However pragmatism reigned and the fact that the new pole held the line the ESB had set down seemed to satisfy him. After what seemed an age, he looked at my mother with a wry smile on his face before telling the workers to pack up and move on.

Despite previous opinions of the man, my mother would never hear a bad word said against him after that. She said the ganger showed after all that he did have a "better nature...even after being outfoxed."

Denis O'Higgins is a native of Knockcroghery, Co Roscommon but now lives in Co Monaghan. Married with a daughter, he is a retired wildlife ranger whose hobbies include writing and travel.

"We received a visit from the parish priest of the time who told us it was improper to have adults appearing without proper attire in our garden."

Miranda Conroy – A Distant Place, Far Beyond The Known World

13

A Distant Place, Far Beyond The Known World

Miranda Conroy

I GREW up in suburban Dublin but our house was totally immersed in 'Rural Electrification'.

Finland where the poles were sourced was indeed 'a distant place, far beyond the known world' of at least Ireland in 1947.

That was due to the fact that my dad, Peter Conroy who was the Divisional Accountant for ESB during the Rural Electrification Scheme, was the person who sourced and bought most of the one million poles for ESB from the inception of the scheme in 1947 to his retirement.

Dad came from an accountancy background but he was really a logistics manager to give it a modern term. In fact he was both Divisional Accountant and Logistics on this scheme, who as Michael Shiel's records in his book 'The Quiet Revolution,' loved the cut and thrust of business.

From the day he was put in charge, he rapidly built an intelligence network regarding the availability and going rates of ships in the pole-supply trade. He quickly developed a reputation among the ship owners in the Baltic trade as Shiel's wrote: "A man who drove a hard bargain and was difficult to hoodwink."

Dad was a raconteur with exceptional inter-personal skills and extremely resourceful.

Both were put to play when I was told the story that long before my time, he was bargaining in Finland and used the Irish language when sending telegrams back to head office. It meant he was the only translator when the answer arrived back – he told the Finnish suppliers that his bosses were not happy and he that he would need better terms of trade between the two countries.

It worked and Dad saved the country substantial amounts at a time when cost was a critical factor in the scheme.

In such circumstances, Finnish business people and ship owners and personnel would often land in Dublin and invariably they would end up being entertained by my mother in our Goatstown home.

Those nights I would be told: "The Finns are coming about the poles."

I would stay up to greet them and receive the Fazer chocolates and feel really special. My dad had a great philosophy in these situations – embrace the Finnish culture. So I grew up surrounded by reindeer skins, Finnish Vodka, Finnish art and design, sculpted Finnish candles, glassware called Ultima Thule – which translates as "a distant place, far beyond the known world."

That too is a reminder of what the novelty of Rural Electrification must have been to the people who got it for the first time in the forties and subsequent decades – it was indeed far beyond the known world.

And then there was the sauna in our back garden, hand made in Finland. We had it specially delivered in 1964 and it became a central element to our back garden.

As I got older and went to school, I would not just tell others that visitors from Finland came to our sauna, but insisted on pronouncing it as they did – sowna. It caused quite a scandal over time as neighbours complained about glimpses of flesh in our garden as users came from the sauna into the house.

We received a visit from the parish priest of the time who told us it was improper to have adults appearing without proper attire in our garden.

Of course the Finnish businessmen couldn't understand our parochial views on the human body.

"What is wrong with nudity?" they would ask incredulously.

The shipping brokers, captains and owners would say it was a way of cleansing the body after a day's work.

My mother, however, would plead with them when they had the

sauna before dinner not to present themselves naked on the veranda and instead dress before crossing into the house.

Obviously the same rules didn't apply when Dad was carrying out work in Finland. We have pictures of him in a business meeting at the side of a lake where he and a colleague were sitting naked as you do when having a Sauna, all in the name of commerce as that was how the Finnish compatriots did business and still do. A bit akin to the deals done on Irish golf courses nowadays.

My mother was an excellent foil for my father in these situations as she was a good cook and a great hostess.

She even kept a book on those we entertained, what they ate and drank and what presents they brought but unfortunately these records have been lost. Which is a pity.

Cloudberry Liqueur made from berries which only grow North of the Arctic Circle were described as 'rocket fuel' and while the Finnish people knew to drink just a thimble of it in our very own Ultima Thule glasses some of the Irish colleagues would get caught out by pouring a liberal measure into deep wine glasses.

Without my knowing it, the Rural Electrification scheme had been at the centre of my falling in love with all things Finnish.

I was so besotted (still am as are my children) with its culture and people that on entering adult life at 18, I went to Finland to mind Virpi, the 18 months-old-baby and granddaughter of my father's friend, Mikko Nahkuri, a relationship formed in the mid 1940s.

Virpi in turn grew up and had a love of Ireland and when she was old enough like her father Jussi who came and stayed with my parents in 1958 and also worked in the ESB for a brief sojourn, she came to stay with me in Dublin. While here, she met and fell in love with a Cavan man, John Luke from Arva.

They set up home here for a while and then both decided to live in Finland with their two daughters.

So over the years we haven't so much built up Finnish friends as Finnish family.

I know my dad felt the same. He was 60 when I was born and one of the things I treasure most is a post card he sent back from Finland to my Mum when I was just two months old.

It is poignant because I think he was very aware that he might not live long enough to see me grow up into adulthood.

On the post card he wrote: "Here in central Finland I heard the cuckoo today for the first time this year and thought of you and Mum ...with loving thoughts, Dad."

His premonition was right as Dad died when I was 12 but he left me a legacy that I will always be grateful for.

It is a bequest beyond riches because it mirrors his own love of Finland, of Finnish people and their culture.

In some ways it is an invisible thread that is still as magical for me as when I was a child looking on as Dad mingled with all the guests of the nation he brought to our house.

My Dad through his work with the Rural Electrification Scheme left me a legacy of magic that is my Finnish family.

Miranda Conroy, MIACO, is the daughter of Peter Conroy, Divisional Accountant ESB during the Rural Electrification Scheme. She lives in Co. Kildare with her two sons.

14

Distemper And Blown Elements

Nancy Power

IT was a two-mile walk to town and of course, a walk two miles back. I often think the return journey must have been hard on my mother because she was carrying with her the big bag of dry mixture for the distemper and, even back then; she was no longer a young woman. It's a notion of the time I write about when I mention distemper. It's difficult nowadays to understand that my mother's only choice of colour that day was green.

Distemper was an early form of whitewash, also used as a medium for artistic painting and usually made from powdered chalk or lime and size (a gelatinous substance). Alternatives to chalk often included toxic white lead. But that thought was of no concern to my mother on this particular occasion. She had a deadline to meet and, even though her load was heavy, her footsteps were quick

Distempered surfaces can be easily marked and discoloured, and could not be washed down, so distemper was best suited to temporary and interior decoration. However my mother knew that the application was quick and that was what she wanted. An instant fix.

Many Medieval and Renaissance painters used distemper painting rather than oil paint for some of their works. My mother read the instructions, mixed the concoction in an old chipped enamel bucket and dipped in her six-inch brush. She was no DaVinci, no Michelangelo, but what she lacked in talent she made up for in enthusiasm.

The previous day she got the word. A man in a collar and tie cycled up to the yard gate and told her that the men were coming in two days to put in 'the light'. The progress of wire and poles across the landscape was creeping ever closer to her cottage. There was great excitement about it locally. The parish priest was encouraging his flock from the altar to modernise. There were opportunities and benefits from the new energy. The community could rise up out of darkness, nothing to be afraid of he told them.

I was working the day she painted the interior of the house. Even before I lifted the hasp on the gate, I could smell the lime from the distemper. She was bent over, washing out the paintbrush when I got inside. There were splashes on the floor, the windowpanes and, of course, on the woman herself.

"What d'ye think of the colour?" She straightened up and supported the small of her neck with both paint-daubed hands. "Its very green," was all I could think of saying. "It'll be grand when it dries out. You can never know with this stuff when it's wet. It might be darker or lighter in shade, but if nothing else it'll be clean looking when the light is shining on it."

In a sense, she was right. The place did look brighter when we threw the brown switch and the plastic lampshade cast illumination all about the kitchen. There wasn't a spider's web to be found and the shadows were banished from the night. It was just the shade of green that was unnatural.

When we eventually got a television, I'd watch Jacques Cousteau programmes and there was a certain watery green hue to some of the undersea photography that echoed back to my mother's choice of distemper shade.

From that day onwards nothing was ever quite the same for her. Electricity would rule her days.

Her finest and worst hour was when she acquired an electric kettle. The magical convenience of being able to boil water without recourse to wood or turf or reluctant kindling was one of her greatest sources of pleasure. There it was at the flick of a switch, tea anytime you wished. And then the hints and tips started filtering in from the locality.

Not alone was the wall limey, but so too was the water. Limescale began to accumulate on the electric element within the kettle. "Put a glass marble in it," insisted one of the neighbours and it will stop the build-up. So after that you would hear the marble rattling about whenever the water boiled.

There was also a strict warning. "Make sure to plug out the kettle whenever it reaches the boil." It had no cut-off switch and if the water level evaporated below the level of the element it would burn out! My mother was very careful in this regard. She'd watch over it and pull the plug at the first moment she'd hear the marble rattling. Then one Sunday morning she came home after Mass. There had been a bitter frost that was slow to lift. The air was raw with an Easterly wind and she was perished with the cold. She never even paused to take off her coat or even her hat (the one with the vicious hatpin), but went straight to the kettle and plugged it in. Perhaps the theme of the sermon distracted her? Or maybe she'd heard a bit of juicy gossip in the churchyard? Who knows, but she forgot to fill the kettle and it boiled dry and blew the element!

She loved her kettle so much, she could not be consoled. I remember her crying bitter tears over the loss of her convenient tea-maker. And even though we assured her that the appliance was repairable, she somehow felt that she had let down the whole spirit of Rural Electrification.

A woman born in 1888, who brought a dozen children into the world and who lived long enough to boil water in a contraption that required neither flame of fire felt such a bond with an inanimate object that she could weep for its injury.

We should have known when we reflected back on the efforts she made to welcome the arrival of 'the light'. We should not have been surprised at the trouble she took to anoint the house and herself with watery green distemper in its honour.

Nancy Power is a longtime committee member of Callan Heritage Society and an active community volunteer in her native town.

"To save power, he would get the men in under the cows milking and then turn off the electric light until they were finished about eight minutes later. He would then briefly turn on the light for them to strain the milk, and turn it off again between each cow milking."

Luke McGuinness – 'Reciting The Angelus To The Chimes Of Big Ben'

Man Power: Eleven men combine to place a pole in position during the roll-out of the Rural Electrification Scheme.

Photographs Courtesy ESB Archives

Ready To Sell: Demonstrators show off the latest in electrical appliances on August 22, 1957.

And They're Off: Erecting the first pole at Kilsallaghan,
Co Dublin on November 5, 1946.

Shortcut: Workers carrying a pole through a ditch in the early
days of the Rural Electrification Scheme.

Look, No Hands! A worker effortlessly climbing to the top of a pole to carry out his duties.

Cable Crew: Workers take a break for a quick photograph behind drums of wire during the Rural Electrification Scheme.

High Wire Etchings: 'The Linesmen', by Cathy Henderson, Artist & Printmaker (Rural Electrication 60th Anniversary 2006 Limited Edition Print, Commissioned by ESB).

Double Up: A crew erecting twin poles to carry high-tension cables.

The Light Brigade: Two workers on a ladder at a house in Dromiskin, Co Louth are watched by school children as they prepare to connect the village up for electricity.

Standing Tall: A worker looks totally at ease thanks to well-designed climbing irons and safety harness.

Getting Connected: ESB employees prepare to bring the power into a remote dwelling.

Big Day For The Town: The electricity arrives at Rosses Point, Co Sligo in November 1947.

DISTRICT	ADDRESS OF DISTRICT OFFICE	COUNTIES COMPRISING DISTRICT
ATHLONE ...	10 Church Street ...	Galway (East), Longford, Offaly, Roscommon (South), Tipperary (North) and Westmeath.
CORK No. 2 ...	Kilbarry	Cork (except North-West).
DUBLIN No. 2 ..	41 Merrion Square	Dublin, Kildare (East), Meath (South) and Wicklow (except extreme South and West).
DUNDALK ...	Chapel Street ...	Cavan, Louth, Meath (North and Central) and Monaghan.
GALWAY ...	Newtownsmyth ...	Galway (except extreme East) and Mayo (South).
LIMERICK ...	41 O'Connell Street	Clare, Cork (extreme North), Limerick (except extreme West) and Tipperary (West and South-West).
PORTLAOIGHISE	Mountrath Road ...	Leix, Kildare (South-West), Wicklow (West), Carlow (North), Kilkenny (North), Tipperary (East).
SLIGO	Castle Street ...	Donegal, Leitrim, Mayo (North), Roscommon (North) & Sligo.
TRALEE	22 Bridge Street ...	Cork (North-West) and Kerry.
WATERFORD ...	Gracedieu Road ...	Kilkenny (South), Tipperary (South-East), Wexford and Wicklow (South), Carlow (South) and Waterford.

ISSUED BY RURAL ELECTRIFICATION OFFICE, ELECTRICITY SUPPLY BOARD, DUBLIN.

RURAL ELECTRIFICATION

- WHAT DOES RURAL ELECTRIFICATION MEAN TO YOU?

- HOW CAN YOU GET IT TO YOUR HOUSE AND FARMYARD?

- HAVE YOU TO PAY FOR THE LINES?

- MUST YOU PAY FOR WIRING YOUR OWN PREMISES?

- WHAT MUST YOU PAY FOR ELECTRICITY?

- HOW CAN ELECTRICITY HELP YOU?

THE ANSWER TO THESE AND OTHER QUESTIONS WILL BE FOUND IN THIS LEAFLET.

Light Offerings: An early ESB advertisement showing how new appliances could help save labour in the household.

15

Reciting The Angelus To The Chimes Of Big Ben

Luke McGuinness

MY first memory of the ESB is from about 1950 when the ESB dropped poles at the side of our road for the erection of a new electricity line in the Meath countryside which took three years to get there.

When my father saw them he went and got an electrician, Frank Maher, from Ratoath to wire our house and yard. Frank had come to live here from Bolton after the Second World War. The poles were part of the main line between Finglas in Dublin and Oldbridge near Drogheda in Louth.

It was the spring of 1953 before the rural scheme arrived but their research found that some houses did not want electricity. When my father heard this he undertook a local canvass to try to change their minds. He had lived in America for a number of years and knew of the benefit of light and power.

Our house was finally connected in July 1953. I remember this was due to happen on the first day of the Bellewstown races. I was so disappointed when we got home and still no light. We went to the races again the next day and this time when we returned and flicked the kitchen switch, we were greeted with a wonderful surprise

With the addition of electricity to our home, the first thing we got was a new electric radio as we were very limited with our old battery one.

At the time we had some men working on the farm milking cows and they would come into our kitchen for supper about nine o'clock.

If our parents were not there, my older sister Mary would turn on the BBC for the striking of Big Ben on the hour.

The two men used to stand up and recite the angelus in Irish. We would have to run out with the laughter. How cruel children can be!

In February, 1956 we got our first television with BBC the only channel available to us. Our neighbours came in regularly to see the horse racing. That first year we had over 30 to see the Grand National race from Aintree. Our big living room could not hold them all, some people had to stand outside and look in through the windows.

Our television also drew big crowds for some of the big races at Cheltenham and we had crowds of women for the wedding of Princess Grace of Monaco.

Although electricity usage was becoming widespread, we still had one neighbour who thought it was very costly. On the dark evenings he still used the old oil lamp. He had two men working on the farm, mainly for milking. To save power, he would get the men in under the cows milking and then turn off the electric light until they were finished about eight minutes later. He would then briefly turn on the light for them to strain the milk, and turn it off again between each cow milking.

This man had a yard which had an outside light. He was very sparing with this light too. One morning he left it on to get work started but later forgot to switch it off for the rest of the day.

The two workmen never mentioned it and it was near dark when the farmer noticed it himself. He asked them had they not seen the light it. They said that they did but thought he had a reason for it.

He was livid with them but funny enough after getting his next ESB bill, he saw it didn't break the bank and after that, he eased back on his battle against the light.

Luke McGuinnes is a self-educated design engineer from Co Meath. He was eight years old when the Rural Electrification first came to his family home.

16

Night Of The Long Count In A Wicklow Village

Con Foley

IT made national headlines the night Knockananna had its big 'switch on' on Aug 13, 1957 – but for all the wrong reasons.

It had been an effort to get the electric in our direction as we did a survey of the people around and were getting nowhere. We also appeared to be a district that was too thinly populated.

Then like everything else, things started to happen in peculiar ways. We heard the ESB lads were in Donard and after making further representations, we had a team in our village and were ready to go six weeks later. The crews worked night and day and before we knew it, we had a committee organizing the biggest single event ever in our village – the electric switch on.

Everyone from around the place made an effort to be part of the occasion. After the dignitaries from the ESB and the Council did their tasks, they sat down with the rest of us to a meal and a dance in the local hall.

At the stroke of midnight, the Tilley Lamps were extinguished and the PP, Fr John Mooney, pressed a switch and the whole village was flooded with light. The event took place to the music of the Blue Diamond Showband while an ad hoc ladies committee provided all who attended with a great supper.

There was great merriment and fun and as the dance came to an end, a number of patrons adjourned to the local taverns to continue the night's celebrations. As the night wore on a note of discord arose between locals and some of the ESB men. General recall is that it stemmed from the arrival of one of the ESB crew who announced to all and sundry that he was "the best bloody man in Knockananna." By daybreak, his claim was in tatters as well as his clothes.

With a lot of drink consumed by then, this proved the spark to light up something else – the longest row in the history of rural electrification. It went from the pub out onto the street and finally came to an end just before daybreak in a cornfield near the bullock ford.

One of those who received quite a few blows was the engineer on the job. He was very good at his work but wasn't everyone's cup of tea. Words borrowed words about how he had treated some fellows in the course of the work and the friction became tangible.

No one shouted stop and what happened next always reminds me of John Wayne fighting as Sean Thornton with Squire 'Red' Will Danaher in the film, 'The Quiet Man.'

Only when the punches were thrown in Knockananna, a great many managed to get involved.

One local had left the dance to walk home a girl shortly before the function ended at 2am.

He tripped back into the village an hour later and fell over a body that had blacked out on the road in which he was travelling. No sooner had he bent down to see what he had tripped over than three or four lads began swinging punches at him. He later said he had the perfect night – a court from a good-looking woman and a fight to round off proceedings.

I was 25 back then – I am 84 now – and I remember being at the dance with my brother. We went home shortly before the fighting broke out. We lived only a few hundred yards from the village. Around 5am we both heard raised voices – a lot of them I might add – and got up. We went back to the village and to our surprise saw the melee at its height.

The poor old engineer got plenty of fight in those small hours. His eyes were both blackened and his jaws reddened to such an extent that even though his work was finished, he stayed on for a few weeks in the place as he didn't want his family to find out what he had been involved in.

He was made feel welcome after the bloodletting... as the event cemented friendships and ended whatever hostilities were between people. Not just ESB and locals, by the time the last box was landed local people who had issues with others from the same area had also aired their grievances.

The wonderful thing about the night is while many of pub going age had black eyes and other visible injuries of combat, not one law case was ever taken.

However, because of the numbers involved and the length of time over which it was carried out, word of mouth leaked it beyond village boundaries. One of the daily newspapers had a heading: 'Pylons bring war to Wicklow village.'

The local newspaper was less verbose in declaring: 'What began as a pleasant function ended up as a good old-fashioned shindy.'

The memory for me of Rural Electrification coming to our part of the world is enshrined in large part in the memory of the fight and its aftermath.

As the weeks passed and the work turned towards harvesting, the only visible reminder of that night was the engineer's shirt that had been pulled off his back and hung high up on a tree in the village.

It remained there for quite a few months as a sort of silent sentinel...

Con Foley is a native of Knockananna and worked on the farm which has been in the family name for five generations. A widower with three children and four grandchildren, he has a great interest in local history and writing.

"Sometimes I looked up to the mountain land where those families survived for generations and think with sadness in my heart that we have lost something forever in that part of the Slieve Blooms."

Paddy Heaney -
A Lament For The Mountain People

17

A Lament For The Mountain People

Paddy Heaney

I WONDER what would have happened to the country if the government hadn't charged the ESB to roll out the Rural Electrification when it did?

How many villages and communities would have found it difficult to remain or perhaps disappeared altogether?

It gave light and power to so many places that allowed people the tools to move into the modern age. However there were places that were either too remote or hadn't the infrastructure like roads or bridges to get to those places and bring light and power to families living there.

I don't blame ESB for this but I would point an accusing finger at successive governments for not putting the infrastructure in.

If they had done that from the time we got our freedom, then the ESB would have been able to get to the place which I cherish and which alas, was by-passed.

I write this with an ache in my heart because despite the hope in our area, the work never went as high up the mountain area around my own people in Cadamstown, Co Offaly.

Every one of the families that had lived there for generations fought for Irish freedom down the centuries. In my opinion they deserved better than being forced to emigrate. There is virtually no trace of their footprints in the mountains now as their small holdings have been planted in forest.

My ancestors lived in the highest point of that area; it must have been a hardy but healthy existence as my grandfather lived to 105.

From walking the area, I dare say it was a lovely place visually to live in and also a healthy way of life.

For hundreds of years, there were 60,000 acres across the Slieve Blooms that had its own farming culture. The people there knew how to create their own fertilizer for crops by using a scraigheen (slean) to cut out mountain sods and pile them up in a heap. They would then burn what they had gathered and use the ashes to spread as fertilizer.

They had their own way of cutting potatoes and corn (oats) ridges into the ground at the higher levels. Indeed the families up there provided the oats for horses in the Crimean War.

The crop was called "black oats" and grew to over six feet in height that as well as selling on to make a living, they used to make stirabout (porridge) for food.

In those times there were no combine harvesters so they would thresh their corn with a flail consisting of three tongues of leather.

The crop would be on the floor and the person flailing would take the grain out of the ear and the chaff would be cast aside.

About 20 years ago, a German man came to live up there and the power was channeled up that way as indeed were roads.

But it came too late for a generation of mountain people – a community of 33 families – who have relocated to England and other parts of the globe at various times over the past three score years ago.

Sometimes I looked up to the mountain land where those families survived for generations by adapting to their surroundings and think with sadness in my heart that we have lost something forever in that part of the Slieve Blooms.

Of course I appreciate that there were limits on where the Rural Electrification could and couldn't go... and at the end of the day I suppose I'm thankful that so many communities have survived and prospered because the electricity came their way.

Paddy Heaney is a native of Cadamstown and is a local historian. His family has been in the Slieve Bloom Mountains area since 1601.

18

Solus Ar Barr Báta
(Light On Top Of A Stick)
Seán Hallinan

T HE air was humid. Only the drone of insects disrupted the veil of uneasy silence that hung over the countryside. Then the thunderstorm broke with an awesome fury. A sharp searing strike of lightening was followed instantly by a colossal clap of thunder.

The lights in our bungalow dimmed and flickered and finally cut out. My young sons raced into the living room. "The telly and play station are gone, Dad," they choroused. "What will we do?"

My mind trolled back more than a half century to the late 1950s when I had experienced that same occurrence for the first time. My Dad had known how to entertain us children. In fact I knew he had positively taken satisfaction from our very first power outage.

Our village and community had been a cauldron of excitement and activity as everyone anticipated "the coming of the light". Months and weeks before, canvassers had trudged the laneways and back roads knocking on doors and exhorting the virtues of the new "electric". The Parish Priest had spoken passionately from the pulpit about the need for progress. "My dear brethren...this new convenience will transform all our lives and will be of great benefit to the school, the hall and the parochial house and each of your homesteads."

Not everyone was convinced. "It will electrify the water and burn the gizzard of man and beast," was one view of what would happen. Such apocalyptic forecasts from village sages and shaman seemed to unduly influence my own father, though to be fair his opposition was in the main, politically motivated.

"Ground Rent... I won't be paying any ground rent!" he declared.

"The rack-renting landlords got away with it for years and we won't be going back to paying that."

Mother with her calm wisdom tried to sooth his concern. "No it won't be like that at all...just a regular repayment we can afford and look at the comforts we will have".

Father retorted: "My father and his father before him had only a rush light, a lantern or a paraffin lamp and that will be good enough for me until ye carry me out that half door".

Mother admonished him: "There will be no one here to carry you out. Your sons will be grown and gone to England and America. What young woman in the future would ever set a step inside this house without the electric? Don't be heeding auld fools who are as tight as tuppence and sign up like the good sensible man you are."

He hesitated, influenced no doubt by her generous praise and she knew in her heart he would not go against her wishes. "Hmm...well we'll see, I might...and then again I might not sign for it. But anyway let the hare sit...let the others take the plunge first. If they can't meet the dues and they have to rear a pig a quarter to pay for it ...I will backslide then me self!"

"You'll not backslide, James," she said firmly. "One thing we never were – were jibbers or backsliders We'll honour our word. God is good and I'll put the eggs towards it."

The work crews and linesmen trundled into the parish. Some had a reputation that preceded them as "ladies men". The PP was extra vigilant in his nightly hedge and haycock patrols after the dances in the Riverside Hall. He organised a Redemptorist Mission in the Parish for the following November and was commended by the bishop for his foresight.

Soon great sturdy poles stood proud like sentries in the hedgerows, sod banks and boundaries. Double cables, a welcome communal perch for scores of crows and starlings, stretched for endless miles.

It was widely boasted that our local workmen were the strongest in the county, the country and indeed the world. Any two men from our parish could carry a pole on their shoulders and erect it unaided.

At the big 'switch-on' there was much revelry as the local PP and

TD turned on the light. The public house was packed to capacity and the hall was wedged for the Céili.

Mary Mooney was agog with the brightness of it and she told all and sundry in the well-lit cloakroom: "Well you know what…I don't know myself when I look in the mirror."

My father, the reluctant disciple, sold off our paraffin table lamp for €5 to a traveller. The lamp, a family heirloom had been purchased years previously by a rich American aunt.

Then the unforeseen happened, a violent thunderstorm erupted and our cottage was suddenly plunged into darkness. My father let out a stream of Gaelic curses as the light went out "Do ainm an deabhal! Nil se ach solus ar barr bátá!"

Mother rummaged for a selection of candles – slightly used baptismal ones, stumps of red candles left over from Christmas, and slim white ones usually used for Baptismal vows at Sodality in the Church.

My father took off his belt, rolled it up and enticed us children. "I bet you can't put a pencil in the exact middle of this." Later with the benefit of flickering candlelight he made a variety of bird and animal silhouette images on the whitewashed walls with thumb and fingers. This first home produced live cartoon show held a memorable magic.

"We are bored, Dad!" strident voices of gloom raised in discord drew me back to the current blackout. I reassured the boys: "Don't worry, I know how to entertain while the lights are out… my old man was a dab hand at that, no worries the – Solus ar barr bátá – will be back!"

Seán Hallinan works in the Museum of Country Life, Turlough Park, Castlebar in Mayo and his hobbies include the GAA and writing.

"There was also a story about a cat being electrocuted (I heard the word "executed" used.) In the smoke-filled cabins of west Wicklow, it was believed that you couldn't wash a light bulb."

Mattie Lennon – Oh For A Penny Ice Cream and The Smell Of Creosote!

Oh For A Penny Ice Cream And The Smell Of Creosote!

Mattie Lennon

IT was Christmas morning 1952 and in the words of the poet, I was 'six Christmases of age?'

My mother held me firmly by the hand on our way to Mass partly I think because she considered me wild. The valley was in darkness save for the candles in the windows to welcome the Redeemer.

It was a scene that was about to change.

Rural electrification was just arriving in Lacken and the surrounding area but had not yet been switched on. After dawn it was possible to see the poles which had stood, complete with insulators, all summer, and were now strung with high-tension cables.

An ESB official had called to the school to complain about the number of insulators which had been the victim of stone throwing. The schoolboys from the townland of Ballinastockan were the prime suspects. Not because they were more destructive than the rest of us but they were better marksmen with a stone or any small missile. If you stood close to an ESB pole and looked up it appeared to be falling, something to do with an illusion caused by the rolling clouds. The term 'optokinetic movement' would have meant very little to the First Communion class of 1952

Not every house opted for the 'lectric light. This was mainly out of economic necessity and the "cups" on the chimney became somewhat of a status symbol. The switch on ceremony was performed in The

Parish Hall, Valleymount, in January 1953 but until then the valley's illumination was confined to candles, oil lamps and the wick-in-a-Bovril-bottle illumination known as a Jack-lamp.

Adult Mass-goers spoke of the well-dressed men in Ford vans who were travelling the district selling everything from irons, to kettles to electric fires.

Conversation in the area was dominated by several fanciful theories. It was claimed that boiling water in an electric kettle "takes all the oxygen out of it."

There was also a story about a cat being electrocuted (I heard the word "executed" used.) In the smoke-filled cabins of west Wicklow it was believed that you couldn't wash a light bulb.

The fact that improved illumination would highlight physical defect was not overlooked. It was rumoured that one elderly farmer who had two daughters of marriageable age but not blessed with film-star looks was heard to say: "We'd better get rid of them two wans before the 'lectric light comes."

One night when such matters were being discussed in a rambling-house Jack Farrell was sitting in the corner. Jack was a Tallaght man who had inherited a small cottage in the area. There were those who would insist that not all of Jack's stories ran parallel with the highest ideals of veracity. Anyway Jack related the following story.

His father farmed in Killenarden at the back of Jobstown. He went for the pension and was asked if he remembered the Big Wind. The Big Wind was on 6th January in 1839 so if Jack's father remembered it, that would leave him over 70 in 1908.

Farrell senior was more than equal to the challenge. According to Jack his father told the pension officer that, on Sunday January 6, 1839, he was sitting at the fire when a squall of wind took the roof straight off the house and it landed somewhere about Kippure.

A pot of potatoes that was hanging on the pot-rack was blown up the chimney and at the top was struck by lightning. The steam that came out of it was a fright to the world and, said Jack: " They were the first potatoes in Ireland to be boiled by electricity."

The specified depth for the main-line poles was six foot two inches.

Local men were employed as labourers and Neddy Cullen, who was vertically challenged – it was said of him that he could play hurling under a bed – was digging a hole in Tim Browe's field. When he was standing in the hole head and shoulders above the ground he uttered the immortal words: "If that hole is not six feet deep my name is not Neddy Cullen."

When the lorry loads of poles began to arrive it was the first time that I had smelled creosote. When they were hoisted by a number of men it was ensured that each pole was parallel with the perpendicular. In the pre-digital age this was achieved with a length of string and a suitable, small piece of Wicklow granite serving as a plumb-bob.

As children we re-enacted everything that we saw the wiremen do during the day. We were digging holes for "poles" and taking our mothers' spools of thread to string "wires."

I can vividly remember the writing on the first, yellow, warning sign that I saw on an ESB pole 64 years ago – Danger. Keep away. It is dangerous to touch the electric wires. Beware of fallen wires.

My old schoolmate, Pat Brennan, brought the "lectric light" out to the shed and his pigsty using wire from a bed spring. No mention of health and safety then. No ordinary household would dream of buying a fridge and for me, and the 27 other juniors in the "little school" it was a day to be remembered when Mrs White brought in a tray from Burke's shop bearing 28 penny ice-creams.

Speaking of smells, Marcel Proust, in 'The Remembrance of Things Past, put it best: "When nothing else subsists from the past, after the people are dead, after the things are scattered ... the smell and taste of things remain poised a long time, like souls ... bearing resiliently, on tiny and almost impalpable drops of their essence, the immense edifice of memory".

Now, when a neighbour is treating his garden fence and the smell of creosote wafts on the summer air, it's no longer the present and I don't have free travel.

It's 1952 and I am, once again, a six-year old in Kylebeg.

Mattie Lennon is a poet, author, folklorist and traditional music aficionado, who lives amongst the Wicklow hills.

"When I was getting married my mother gave me one of the patched blankets as a reminder of our first electric blanket and our narrow escape from being burned in our beds."

Rita O'Neill – A Narrow Escape With The First Electric Blanket

20

A Narrow Escape With First Electric Blanket

Rita O'Neill

MY late father was a shopkeeper with an enquiring mind and was always fascinated with anything new. With the launch of the rural electrification he became very interested in plugs, switches, junction boxes etc. He said he was going to learn all about it from the book he bought.

In his business he relied on his window display to entice customers into the shop. In winter time the window often got fogged up so that the customers couldn't see the bargains on offer. As an amateur electrician, he bought an electric heating bar, placed it in the window in front near the glass, plugged it in and – no more fogging. Eureka!

Our house was three-storeyed and my parents slept in one of the bedrooms at the very top. In the days before central heating, it was arctic in winter at the top of the house. As children, we joked with hot water bottles in hand that we were going to the North Pole when going to bed.

One evening my father got one of his brilliant ideas: "Sure, if the electric bar worked in the window, why wouldn't it heat the bed?" So he placed it in the bed under the five Foxford blankets, plugged it in. "We'll have a lovely warm bed tonight," he said.

However when my mother opened the bedroom door, she was nearly suffocated with smoke. Her lovely blankets had a brown singed line across them and the mattress was smouldering.

She was so cross with my father and his bright ideas. The smell of burning and smoke was in the house for ages.

Instead of everything being thrown out, my mother used one of the blankets to patch the others, but the brown marks were still a little visible.

When I was getting married my mother gave me one of the patched blankets as a reminder of our first electric blanket and our narrow escape from being burned in our beds.

Rita O'Neill is a former schoolteacher who is a leading member of the Callan Heritage Society and a native of Co Kilkenny.

21

When Your Politics Was Known By The Make Of Your Radio

Agnes Coughlan

HOW many Woobines were smoked or pipes filled with plug tobacco talking about rural electrification we will never know? One thing we do know however, is that the scheme changed the course of our history as a people and a nation.

Down in Clare in particular, DeV held the country people enthralled as he proclaimed the good tidings of a new-age power while a few of the more adventurous souls went up to Ardnacrusha to see what in the name of God was going on.

Old people walked feebly from their chairs and firesides to inspect the miracle as it progressed on the way to flicking the switch instead of lighting the lamp.

I remember that September night we used the switch for the first time – it was strange, almost like living in someone else's house.

Everything looked different in this curious world of blinding light; even the yellow flitches of bacon hanging from the rafters seemed changed under the glare of a hundred watt bulb.

Bulbs of a lesser wattage were installed in the bedroom and parlour while the backroom for storage went without altogether.

For young girls, it was a delight as they could see clearly what they were doing during the Sunday night ritual of getting ready for the dance. For those staying at home on such occasions, the advent of light was quickly followed by power. This meant that radios could be plugged in for use instead of relying on dry batteries.

I remember when our Philips model arrived in a strong box wrapped in newspaper and tied with a grass cord.

As I recall, the brand of radio one purchased had a lot to do with your political beliefs.

If you were a Fianna Fail person who backed DeV, you chose a Philips while according to conventional wisdom, the Blueshirts invariably opted for Bush wirelesses.

Whatever the brand, the new arrivals were all accorded the status of a first born child in each house. Invariably installed on a high press in a freshly cleared corner of the kitchen, there was a threadbare hand-embroidered flour bag to blanket it comfortably when it was not in use.

It opened a new world, Radio Eireann via the Athlone transmitter was a leap into the unknown, while there was news in all sorts of languages if you kept twisting the dials.

Saturday nights became a rush as everyone wanted to have faces washed and curlers in and shoes polished for first mass the next morning before Ceili House came on.

Michael O'Hehir's Sunday broadcasts quickly became as much a Sunday fixture as Sunday dinner and Mass and Holy Communion.

The disgust at DeV's defeat in a general election was summed up in broadcasting terms by a Fianna Fáil supporter who described the glee of a 'Blueshirt' neighbour this way: "Oh, she's above under the Bush crowing".

But there were other more cosmopolitan references. At some stage in the early days of space exploration, we had a terrier named Sputnik and there was also a contrary old ram who revelled in the grand old title of Mr Kruschev. Times indeed were a changing...

Another milestone of change came when a returned Yank caused a major stir when she bought an electric cooker for her home. Men and women arranged visits from miles around to see the wonder of it all while keeping vigil as the cooker baked not one but two cakes of bread at a time.

They all agreed... modern Ireland had arrived.

Agnes Coughlan is from Clonreddan not far from the chapel gates in Cooraclare, Co Clare. She enjoys nature and the simple things in life.

22

Little Volcanoes
Maeve Edwards

H E couldn't resist telling him. He just couldn't. But he'd be damned if he'd let him go off to his grave without letting him know. All day long it had been playing around in his head, and all day long, he'd resisted it.

And all day long too there was a stirring of something coming from inside him, like when the porridge pot on the range began its slow simmer, those puffs of steam rising to the surface in a slow motion eruption.

As a child, he'd stood in this very same place, stirring the porridge pot and waiting for those little volcanoes to rise to the surface.

If he'd had a different life, he might have recognised that the new emotion he felt was joy. Just the stirrings of it now, but joy nonetheless, subdued and restrained though it might be.

"He'll be gone by nightfall, Tom," the doctor said when he came out of the room on the other side of the hearth. He hadn't joined him at his brother's bedside, waiting instead at the kitchen sink with Laddie by his side. The dog knew something was up. He pressed himself close against Tom and waited too for the doctor's footfall against the stone floor.

"You sure have the place ship shape," said the doctor now as he looked around the room. His eyes rested on the dresser, the book shelf in the corner, the black kettle humming on the range, the loaf of bread bought this morning in Curley's down at the crossroads.

Tom knew that the doctor, for all his kindness, would not be able to resist it either, even though he and Ned were no longer a laughing stock in the village. Now they were just a local enigma, pointed out at Mass when newcomers or summer visitors came to stay.

"See those two old men over there? Yes, those two in the caps and shiny boots, they never got the electricity in."

"You're joking!"

"As true as I'm sitting here. They live in a cottage at the bottom of the hill with oil lamps and a transistor radio, the whitewashed one with the blue windows."

"Did someone never tell them the year is 2016?"

"Well they say that Ned, he's the one with the mass of white hair, won't allow his brother get it in."

And the story would be lost in the after mass confusion of buying the Sunday papers and no one would notice as the two old men left the church and headed back down the hill on foot.

No one only a local would notice either that no electric cable ran from the black pole outside their gate to the gable end of the house. And if one of the brothers invited you in and it was summer time, you wouldn't notice either, for the light slanted in through the kitchen window in a quite lovely way, and lit up the room better than any electric light ever could. Or that's what Ned used to say, when one by one the other brothers and sisters left home for America or England, and mother and father passed away in the very room where Ned now lay.

"You can get the electricity in now Tom," the doctor said. "Move yourself into the 21st century." Tom threw a sod of turf on the fire and said nothing.

When the doctor had gone, Tom lifted his eyes to the pole outside the window. Father had objected when it went in at that spot. "It obstructs my view of the hill," he told the men. That was just after the war when the electricity poles came stalking like sentinels across the fields.

But the men wouldn't move it.

"It'll be there waiting for you when you want the electric," the men said. "Over my dead body," he'd said. "It'll be the ruin of the country, that electricity."

Each home on their side of the hill was illuminated one by one, and Tom was in his friend Patrick's house when the light was switched on for the first time. They were eight years old, and filled with excitement as the electric cables were attached to homes across the parish, lighting up corners that had never before seen light.

Tom's mother knew pleading with her husband would get her nowhere. She pursed her lips in that way she had and life continued as normal in the McEvoy household. In truth, the coming of the electricity hadn't changed the lives of their neighbours very much.

It was years before anyone even thought of buying one of those new-fangled washing machines with a roller on the back. And another decade would pass before the first fridge arrived to the area, bringing disbelief in its wake at the taste of milk poured cool from the jug.

And as for automated milking machines, it was the sixties before that happened. No, life had continued on their farm just like it always had. The oil lamps did them just fine, even though as a child, Tom felt a certain shame when his school friends laughed at him. "The McEvoy's don't even have a light switch."

But he'd got used to it.

And Tom had been left behind too. His friend Patrick had gone to work in the Civil Service in Dublin and any joy he'd felt up till then had gone with him. Ned and he were left to live out their lives together.

Ned took after his father. "Over my dead body," the older brother said the last time Tom broached the subject.

Ned stuck to the fields and their sheep farm and Tom looked after the home and the vegetable garden. Like an old married couple they were, without the comfort or the friendship, though God knows there wasn't much of that in their parents' lifetime either.

Tom learnt to rely only on himself. He'd no use for anyone or anything. Once he had his dog by his side, he was alright. But often on winter nights, as Ned and he sat silently by the fire, tuned into the tinny sound of the transistor radio, he'd look over at his bookshelves and long for a time when the electric light would lift the gloom.

By early evening Ned's breathing had changed. He's dying of old age, Tom thought, just like I will when my time comes. His brother's hands lay clasped in front of him, his pyjamas opened at the neck. Mrs Power had come in twice a day to help wash and turn him. He knew she went home with stories. "That old man doesn't deserve to have a brother who cares for him like he does." Tom didn't mind what anyone thought, he would do his duty, just like he always had.

And then he said it. The words came out of his mouth unbidden, surprising even himself at the intensity of their resolve.

"I'm getting in the electricity when you go, Ned!"

Ned's eyes opened wide and his breathing faltered for a moment. But Tom didn't wait for any further reaction. He turned to look at the electricity pole outside the window. It seemed to shine in the early evening light, and he imagined raindrops slipping and sliding down the black cable as it made its way to the gable end of his house.

Maeve Edwards is a native of Clontarf, Dublin but now lives in Bray, Co Wicklow. A mother of two, her writings have been shortlisted for a number of awards.

23

Switch On At Pearse's Cottage

Mattie Nee

I HAD just begun attending school at the 'Tech' in Gort Mór, Rosmuc, which was almost directly across the road from Pádraic Pearse's cottage.

Up to then in 1954 we did our homework with the aid of light from an oil lamp. However, the ESB's 'new scheme' was headed our way and it was the talk of the whole place.

A massive crowd gathered for the big 'switch on' at the gable end of Pearse's cottage. I was there with my mother and father and it's an occasion I will never forget.

The event was held late in the evening and we were surprised and delighted that Éamon de Valera and Pádraig Pearse's sister were among the dignatories who attended for the great occasion.

The speeches were delivered 'as gaeilge.' Then Dev pulled the lever to switch on the electricity to 'all Connemara.'

What a moment! The lights went on all over in the windows of the small whitewashed cottages. I couldn't help but think of the words... 'and then there was light.' It was truly a night of nights for us all.

Even though Pearse's cottage wasn't connected to the main line at this time, the ESB built a temporary connecting line to the gable end for the ceremonial switching on of the light.

However, the seven temporary poles were taken down a few days after the visit by the dignatories.

It was many years later – in 1978 in fact, when I was working in Clifden that we finally installed electricity into Pearse's cottage.

He was one of the Irish heroes and I felt it was an honour that I was responsible for giving him the light that year.

Mattie Nee is a native speaker from Rosmuc, Co Galway and a former ESB employee for over 30 years.

24

Vanishing Dust At The Poor Man's Castle

Lorna Sixsmith

G ARRENDENNY Castle – tall and grey, nestled amongst beech and ash trees, and 400 yards up a steep winding lane from the main road – had few near neighbours yet was within three miles of the most heavily inhabited area in rural Ireland.

The small towns of Moneenroe and Castlecomer were densely populated with the hundreds of families working in the coalmines. Many boys left school and spent their whole working lives in the mines, earning multiples of what they would have earned as farm labourers.

Coal had also been extracted from opencast mines on Sixsmith land, a mile from Garrendenny. Although Sixsmiths have been farmers for generations, the first of us to come to this area was a Yorkshireman – an engineer experienced in opencast mining.

Garrendenny was rather a poor man's castle. Its original three-storey section was two-up, two-down with one room in the middle: the kitchen and breakfast room on the ground floor, a huge bedroom known as the dormitory on the first floor, and two small bedrooms at the top, linked by a wooden staircase in a stone tower.

A two-storey extension housed a sitting room, dining room, hall, stairs and three bedrooms. With eight children and four adults living there in 1949, anything that could help with the workload was going to be welcomed.

Electricity was available in Moneenroe in 1949 to serve the coalmines and the large number of people living there. However,

Garrendenny Farm was not considered "economical" enough for the ESB to run poles across to us, over the border in Co Laois. Some farming neighbours were fortunate enough to get electricity installed but we were still half a mile too far away. My grandfather campaigned hard but it was fruitless until the ESB decided to run electricity to a coalmine further up the hill in Kilgorey. Only three fields across from Garrendenny, and with a ground rent of £14 per annum, finally we were considered to be "an economical farm".

My grandfather, of course, wanted the electricity for the yard. The 14 cows that had been hand milked could now be milked with the bucket plant, two at a time, within the little cow houses. The advent of electricity allowed him to expand the herd to 21 cows.

However, there was a limit to the number of months they could be milked by machine. Electricity helped to save labour with another task: that of cutting up the turnips to feed the livestock. The problem was there was only one motor. From November to March, the motor was taken off the milking machine and put on the turnip cutter while the cows went back to being milked by hand. This went on for years, and I wonder now why they didn't purchase a second motor.

Farming neighbours learnt how to become "electricians" and extended the wires to my grandfather's other sheds in return for 50 cigarettes a shed. In this way, eventually all the sheds in the yard had electric light. There was another advantage to having electricity in the yard (or perhaps it was a disadvantage): work could finish later.

Before electricity, cows had to be milked by 5pm in the winter before complete darkness fell; now they could be milked later if other work was delayed.

The differences electricity made in the house were immense and my grandparents invested in a number of labour-saving devices within those first few years of getting electricity. All rooms, even the attic bedrooms, had electric light. Instead of heating flat irons by the fire, an electric iron was plugged in. Instead of trying to regulate a fire in a range cooker, they could set the correct temperature on the electric oven. Weekends were always busy at Garrendenny as, with numerous visitors calling on Sunday afternoons, Saturdays were spent baking. Eight apple tarts were baked every Saturday and not a crumb was left by Sunday evening. How my grandmother must have loved her electric oven.

Rather than scrubbing dirty clothes in a tub every Monday, the washing machine was used. Piped water didn't arrive until 1964 and so buckets of water still had to be carried in from a tap in the yard, but the washing machine heated the water and washed the clothes. The washing machine had a wringer on top of it so the clothes didn't have to be wrung out with bare hands any more.

A refrigerator was also purchased. My grandmother was grateful for being able to store food for longer, but for the eight children in the family the highlight was that a large block of ice cream could be purchased from the local shop and stored in the icebox for a Saturday night treat.

And then, in 1950, there was the evening the travelling salesman called. The rat-a-tat-tat from the knocker on the front door was unusual enough, as most neighbours called to the back door. When my grandmother opened the door onto the dusk, she was confronted with a dapper little man with a black moustache, wearing a black suit. He lifted his hat as he introduced himself. He wanted to demonstrate how an Electrolux vacuum cleaner worked. He came with some provenance as he had just sold one to a neighbour.

He was ushered into the sitting room, this guest of great consequence. If he had just sold a vacuum cleaner to Mrs L, he wasn't going to be brought to the kitchen. Standards had to be upheld and there was a carpet and fire in the sitting room.

He asked for an assistant to help him demonstrate the power and skill of this pale blue sausage-shaped vacuum cleaner, an invention that would render the brooms redundant, make the curtains and carpets beam with colour and ban cobwebs and dust if used regularly. One of the older girls, 15, finished school but not yet "serving her time" in a shop away from home, was nominated to be chief assistant. She was particularly enthusiastic as it was her job to dust and sweep this three-storey dwelling with its two staircases.

My grandmother and grandfather sat on the sofa, my great grandfather on an armchair, the 22-year-old labourer on a stool and my father and his other six brothers and sisters knelt on the carpet in a semi-circle.

The salesman stroked the pale blue and silver vacuum cleaner almost reverently with his pale, thin, long fingers; a contrast to the red, gnarled and calloused hands of the other adults in the room. He traced the word Electrolux with his fingers, bringing attention to the raised silver letters stamped against the red background.

He asked for an old newspaper and shook out a double page, laying it carefully on the carpet as if it were a small picnic rug, unfurling a corner and straightening a crease. He unpacked the hose from its bag; snakelike, it furled around the rug with its cleaning head resting against the hearth.

Opening up one end of the vacuum cleaner, he let each of the children take a turn to peer into it and then he shook it over the newspapers. Tiny fragments of dust fell out. "You can see it is completely empty," he explained, "and I'll show you just how much dust it will suck up shortly."

The 15-year-old ran to plug in the lead while he slotted the hose into one end of the vacuum cleaner. Taking the cleaning head off and with almost majestic poise, he flicked the switch. The cleaner revved up and he placed the nozzle near to the back of the hand of each child so they could feel the suction.

He then did the same with the adults. Switching off the machine for a moment, he replaced the cleaning head, pressed the black button again and pushed the brush along the carpet. The children leaned forward; would the whole carpet be sucked into that hose? Was there going to be a transformation? Yes! The carpet's colours were brighter, the design was clearer; the pile in the carpet had risen.

The salesman let his assistant take over and she vacuumed the area in front of the fireplace. When she had completed that, he told her to unplug the lead and he removed the hose from the canister. He walked over to the newspaper and opened the canister.

Out poured grey dust, hair and carpet fibres to lie in a neat pyramid on the black and white paper. All he needed to do was mention that it could be paid for with easy payments once a month and it was a sale.

Some neighbours didn't get an electricity connection until the mid-1960s and one neighbour, 500 yards higher on the hill behind us, still didn't have it in 1981 when he sold the farm. The coalmine at Kilgorey was worked for less than a year, yet my grandparents were always grateful to it as otherwise it would have been at least another decade before electricity arrived at Garrendenny.

Lorna Sixsmith farms at Garrendenny with her husband Brian James and their two children. She is the author of three books: Would You Marry A Farmer? How To Be A Perfect Farm Wife and her latest best-seller, An Ideal Farm Husband.

"At the spring and autumn equinoxes, they had these caves or cairns so carefully constructed that the light from the sun would penetrate the darkness of the cave and shine to the far end of it."

**Declan Coyle –
Dungimmon, Light Years Ahead**

25

Dungimmon –
Light Years Ahead

Declan Coyle

I COME from an area that for centuries has understood the importance of light more than most.

Dungimmon in Co Cavan is a townland perfectly placed in a lovely valley between Slieve Na Calliagh (Loughcrew), the Mountain of the Holy Healing Woman and the romantic lake of Lough Sheelin which is forever linked to the love story of Orwin and Sabina.

Thousands and thousands of years ago the engineers from Dungimmon and the surrounding areas built special caves on the holy hillside. They were incredible geniuses.

At the spring and autumn equinoxes, they had these caves or cairns so carefully constructed that the light from the sun would penetrate the darkness of the cave and shine to the far end of it.

They even marked the movements of the sun throughout the day with sun symbols. They had other beautiful drawings carved on the walls of the cave. Long before the Carpenter Poet of Galilee spoke of these things, the people from Dungimmon, Ballinacree, Oldcastle and Ballinlough knew that light overcomes all darkness. My neighbours were the original 'it's better to light a candle than to curse the darkness' people.

Some thousands of years later St Patrick came and lit his famous Paschal Fire on the hill of Slane. The king and his courtiers saw the fire from the Hill of Tara and the ruler wondered: "Who is this light-bringer?"

Patrick later met the king and they had a fantastic theological conversation over a light lunch of salmon from the Boyne and a local salad washed down by some frothy goblets of local Meath mead. He explained that he wanted to bring light to every corner of Ireland and the King gave him his blessing to do so.

Patrick did a great job but one man can only do so much. He needed the help of the ESB's rural electrification scheme to complete his light mission.

Before they set out on that expedition in the middle of the last century, the people still had to fight the dark with limited resources.

"Light the lamp," someone would shout in our house. On dark evenings in the fifties this would propel Mammy into action. She'd roll a piece of newspaper, put it into the fire and firstly light her cigarette before using it to light the kitchen lamp.

It was either flickering candles or paraffin oil lamps that we depended on for light. Later on we got Tilley paraffin lamps with a pump on the side to inject oil to a white ball-like wick. As the light began to dim, Daddy would order: "Give that lamp a pump."

Around 1957 the 'electric' came and it was transformational. Not only with light but fridges, washing machines and milking machines.

Baths with hot water were installed with the famous immersion switch. The 'sink' switch was okay we were told, but put it to 'bath' and financial ruin was just over the horizon for the household. The famous rhetorical question was never far away: "Do you think money grows on trees?"

Ollie Brogan, the Managing Director of ESB International spoke recently on radio about the incredible success of the company overseas. He paid tribute to the Irish missionaries in Africa who built up the trust and the goodwill that helped him seal many major deals when he was up against intense international competition.

The light of the Gospel paved the way for the light of the ESB. Ollie often told me that the story of how Ireland accelerated its development with the rural electrification is one that resonates deep in the hearts of African leaders.

The roll out of electricity to the far corners of Ireland by the state is a model of development for many African countries. Not just a company cherry-picking the most profitable towns and ignoring the rest. A total roll out which came our way in the fifties.

The light and darkness theme resonated that Christmas at another level in our valley of Dungimmon. I remember Mass in Ballinacree hearing the words: "The people that walked in the darkness have seen a great light."

One man walking out of the church after mass was heard to say to another at the holy water font: "Was the PP referring to the 'Man Above' or the 'Rural Scheme' when he was preaching about the light?'"

The other replied blessed himself slowly before replying: "Knowing him, I'd say he was covering both bases!"

Declan Coyle is a well-known international motivational speaker who is also a best-selling author with his book 'The Green Platform' and his recently published follow-up 'Living The Green Platform'. A former Columban missionary, he played football with Cavan and is married with three children.

"Possibly to tease my mother a little, he would claim that the best cup of tea he had ever been served was in a field, in one of the glass or ceramic insulators used to carry the live wires safely across the newly erected poles."

**Antony Suttle –
Lighting Up The Interior**

26

Lighting Up
The Interior

Antony Suttle

I T could be said that after the drama and tragedies of our achievement of Independence and the subsequent civil war, the most transformative events in Ireland's history as a nation in the 20th century, were rural electrification, the arrival of Telefís Eireann and our joining the EEC (as it was) in 1973.

The first of these, Rural Electrification in Ireland, formed a backdrop to my childhood. Fairly shortly after his leaving school, in the late 1920s, my father had joined the recently created Public Relations Department of ESB.

So, while living in a fully electrified house in suburban Dublin, I grew up listening to my parents conversations on his work in the ESB offices on Merrion Square, then a row of converted Georgian houses. My only childhood exposure to a pre-electric world was occasional holidays with a spinster grand-aunt, Lizzie Kelly, who lived on a small, 40 acre farm in Kildare, about 30 miles from Dublin. There, as a child, I occasionally experienced cooking on hook-hung pots over the fire, oil lamps and bedside candles, and a waterless outside lavatory.

While there had been some limited use of electric power during the late 1800s, primarily for public lighting and tramway systems, it was largely restricted to the larger urban areas. This changed in the late 1920s, with the brave decision by the then government of the new State to commit to developing a large-scale hydro-electric generating plant on the Shannon at Ardnacrusha, which would have the capacity to provide power across all of Ireland.

To justify the expenditure on generating vast supplies of this new power source, an immediate objective for the ESB was to create a demand, by persuading people, firstly to install electricity, and then to buy lots of electric equipment, both for the home and for use on farming and in industry. That would be task of my father and his colleagues in the ESB's Public Relations Department.

As part of that process, the ESB established showrooms around the country, initially in Dublin and the main urban areas. In the showrooms, as in their press advertising, and all of their advisory and promotional leaflets and display stands at the RDS and other shows, the "look" the ESB presented was one of a crisp, clean-lined Modernism, in line with the nature of the new energy source they were providing.

My father's first job in the ESB's PR Department was as a window-display artist for the showrooms. At the time, the ESB and the Brown Thomas department store on Grafton St. were the only commercial premises using professionals for their window displays.

As part of keeping up with overall design trends my father's room was full of back-issues of the Swiss-produced graphic design journal Graphis, and more to my interest, the then more exotic American and British popular magazines, such as Saturday Evening Post, Life, Picture Post, to allow him to follow contemporary consumer-goods advertising.

He had a large drawing board in his bedroom, and would bring work home. I'd watch occasionally as he drafted brochures and layouts for posters. He had developed his interest in typography and lettering by attending night classes at Dublin's College of Art (now NCAD) with the Dutch-trained Professor Romein, also taking life-drawing classes given by Seán Keating.

In 1947 the ESB started the Rural Electrification Scheme. Occasionally he would leave home for a few days to accompany one of the ESB's staff photographer's to capture images of the linesmen wiring the nation. Possibly to tease my mother a little, he would claim that the best cup of tea he had ever been served was in a field, in one of the glass or ceramic insulators used to carry the live wires safely across the newly erected poles.

Sometimes, for shorter trips nearer to Dublin, I would be taken along, in the back of the car, one of the ESB fleet (my father didn't drive), and would accompany him and the photographer as they recorded electricity in use in the many small industries emerging in Ireland's still "protected" economy. One of the ESB drivers, Tommy Brennan, a lovely man, became a personal friend of my father's, and of the rest of us. He minded my father well.

In time, he moved away from his graphic activities and to more direct Public Relations activities, which involved a lot of contact with journalists, both local and from overseas. He became friendly with the Irish Times journalist, Seamus Kelly, then writing the Irishman's Diary column. Together with Patrick Kavanagh, Brian Ó Nuallain, Niall Montgomery and others, they went on, in their spare time, to start the now well developed James Joyce celebrations around the Sandycove tower and Bloom's Day.

My father always had a great love of art in general, and I now realise, a wide self-taught knowledge of painters of all periods, with an advanced awareness, for the Dublin of his time, of modern art. He had a particular interest in the French artist Raoul Dufy (1877-1953), partly because he like to refer him to as the "rale Duffy" and possibly because one of Dufy's major works was a large mural, "The Electric Fairy", commissioned by the Electricity Company of Paris, for the 1937 International Exhibition, celebrating electricity (now in the Paris Museum of Modern Art).

Although I feel he never fully developed his capability, my father was a good draughtsman. He had been advised by Romein, his teacher at the College of Art, to take up sketching, to "loosen his approach". He did so, particularly during the War years, when the activities of the ESB were somewhat curtailed due to shortages. My siblings and I share a number of his sketch books from this period, including some of the views from the back of the Georgian building in which he worked.

In that context, I find it odd that I have no memory of his ever having mentioned the work by his other occasional teacher, of life drawing, Seán Keating, in recording the building of the hydro electric dam at Ardnacrusha. Having attended Keating's evening classes, my father obviously felt he knew him well enough to ask him to make a charcoal portrait drawing of my mother, I think before I was born, but of which I am currently the guardian.

As Dr. Éimear O'Connor indicates in her writings on Seán Keating, and his work on recording the building of Ardnacrusha, he was not commissioned by the ESB, or any other body to do so. Possibly motivated by the fact that the project was close to his birthplace, Limerick, and also illustrated his view of a modern, progressive Ireland, he made his own decision that it should be recorded for posterity. Keating's superiors at both the College of Art and the Department of Education were unsupportive of his idea, and Keating, busy on other projects at the time, had to manoeuvre time off, and organise access to the Ardancrusha site to achieve his objectives.

Today, looking back, I have four sets of visual reminders of that time. Copies of old ESB publicity materials, now looking dated; access to Keating's paintings, at occasional exhibitions and as illustrations in Dr. O'Connor's books on Keating; Keating's portrait of my mother; and my father's sketches of his Georgian workplace on Merrion Square.

Of all of them, it is my father's sketchbooks that I find bring me back to the mid 20th century. In a small back office, a contribution was being made towards a brighter Ireland.

Antony Suttle is an art historian, lecturer and poet from Dublin who likes nothing better than 'looking at pictures'.

27

Singing In The Rain
Noel Mulcahy

I 'D just finished first year engineering at UCD and needed a job. An interview with the deputy Chief Engineer of the ESB in Limerick got me one as a labourer, albeit to do engineering work.

Getting about three pounds, fourteen and sixpence a week felt like a fortune. I could now go on a planned trip to Kerry with a student colleague whose father was willing to lend us his car.

I was assigned to a Rural Electrification area that was just commencing where the lads picked me up in the van every morning. I was authorised to take out a theodolite from the ESB Dockland store and taught myself how to use it as I hadn't reached that level of surveying on my college course.

I spent a week being trained by David Reynolds who was the Rural Area engineer for the Rathkeale area. On the first evening we were at a gathering in his house, there were sandwiches, music and two lovely sisters. Clearly there was more to rural electrification than technology. David explained the philosophy and background of the project. Mr Roe, deputy Chief Engineer of the ESB had designed a nationwide scheme to provide electricity to homes and industrial units.

My job was to establish the backbone line by placing pegs 80 metres apart in a straight line across the area. I sweated bricks trying to maintain the straight aspect; the maps could be faulty, houses not recorded, new afforestation, etc. Two labourers were assigned to me. They used slashers (long-handled billhooks) to cut gaps in the hedges to allow the theodolite to see through the hedges and create the famous straight line.

I was very much at home on a farm after spending many summers on my cousin's in Birdhill. I knew how to watch out for bulls. I could also talk to farming people except, of course, the ones who did not accept that the notice served on them by my predecessor entitled us to legally cross their land, whether they liked it or not.

Danger followed our daily endeavours. One day I'd just set up my theodolite position at the start of the Kildimo area backbone line; my slashers men aligning themselves ready to cut a gap in the hedge for my sight line. I steadied myself with the ranging rod I always carried with me (for protection as much as anything else).

"Look out," my colleague shouted, "there's a bull running towards you."

I ran. My speed to the safety of the nearest gate was of Olympian standard. I learnt my first lesson, always look before you enter a field.

On the Kildimo run I was joined by an ESB map-man, Eddie O'Neill. He and I loved to sing. When It rained we'd dive for the nearest sheltered ditch for cover. And that was where we sang, in a ditch in the rain. At that time 'Ghost riders in the Sky' was a big hit. We perfected it in the ditches of Kildimo. That was the beginning of a special singing relationship with Eddie. Before long we extended our repertoire to operatic arias. His was a baritone voice, mine a tenor. We even managed a tolerable version of the duet from the Pearl fishers on some damp days.

Fourteen years later, we shared the stage for a run of Strauss's 'Die Fledermaus' 14 years later. I played the lead and Eddie played the jail governor.

Customers had visits from cooking advisors to show farmers' wives how to use hobs and ovens. The occasion of a public demonstration in a local hall provided celebration for our team. It was an excuse for food and a bit of a hooley.

Occasionally, some people were not happy to get the electricity. I remember I was carefully walking through the drills of a large cabbage field when an irate farmer came after me with an axe in his hand. I took off up to the nearest boreen and was lucky enough to hail a passing car.

The car I stopped was remarkable. Amazingly, my saviour was a Yank known as the Baron Handley who drove around in a big car with the tricolour painted on it.

The same man offered $50 Million to the Queen of England to buy the Six Counties which he planned to offer to the Irish state. What a thought!

Having finished my second year in college, I got my old job back for the Newcastle West electrification scheme. It was the holy year of 1950 and the district Engineer, Mr. Dooley was on a visit to Rome.

I was asked to open up the area; get an office, hire staff, and get started on the 10KV backbone line. I arranged digs locally. I felt like a king with all my new responsibilities.

The experiences from Kildimo were repeated. By the time I returned to UCD that year, Rural Electrification was well under way. My backbone line terminated with a major distribution pole at the Killarney crossroads. It was christened 'The Killarney Pole' and I am told it is still called that.

As we approached Christmas in 1950, I got a call to University Hall, Hatch Street, Dublin. It was engineer Dooley inviting me to the energising of the 'Killarney pole' and my backbone line. A big party was planned. The team had sent the hat around to cover my expenses. I was so excited. But on the radio the following morning my world was shattered by the news that Mr. Dooley died in a crash on the way home to his people in Roscrea on an icy road.

He was my mentor. His death was a terrible shock to me.

Fear cneasta mar dhuine, eifeacht mar ingiltoir. I shall never forget him.

It was a sad ending to two years of personal development for a budding engineer. Rural Electrification had a huge influence on me. I learned what national strategies were about.

Professor Noel Mulcahy is a retired vice-president of the University of Limerick, a former member of Seanad Eireann and a leading light of the Irish Management Institute.

"Each bucket of water had to be fought for and won. It required you to kneel on the mossy flagstones, skim the water beetles, dragonflies, pond skaters from the glassy surface and then dip the bucket in to receive the benediction of water."

**Áine Nic Liam -
Dowsing For Sweet Water**

28

Dowsing For Sweet Water

Áine Nic Liam

D OWSING for water; attempting with hazel twigs and divining rods to locate ground water sources is an activity that seems to attract more supernatural than scientific response.

One of its early usages was as a locator of metals and dead bodies. As early as 1518 Martin Luther listed dowsing as an act that broke the first commandment. His notion was that divination below the earth invoked occultism.

When the diviner came to my late uncle's house in Co. Mayo to locate a water source he may not have been treated as someone who had sold his soul to the dark forces but definitely he was regarded as a man who possessed powers beyond the gift of ordinary mortals.

Electricity was changing the countryside. Lights were visible now in the nightscape where there were none before and this time there was an explanation. It was nothing to be afraid of. It was innovative science and nothing to do with ghosts or spirits, or spectres.

Before the arrival of Rural Electrification, anyone who wanted water for washing, for drinking or cooking or the multiple other requirements for this essential element had to draw it from the well. The original builders of my uncle's property sited the well on high ground a ways back from the dwelling place. Perhaps this was to avoid contamination or perhaps it was the location where the strongest or most prolific spring was believed to exist. You walked from the kitchen to the front door, through the cobbled yard, around the corner past the bull-house, through the orchard, up the back haggard and through the nearest field to get to the sweet spring well.

Each bucket of water had to be fought for and won. It required you to kneel on the mossy flagstones, skim the water beetles, dragonflies, pond skaters from the glassy surface and then dip the bucket in to receive the benediction of water. My memory is of its cold freshness even in the high-heat days of summer. The shock of the temperature change and the fascination when your hands dipped below the surface and watched the optical distortion was something never forgotten. It was a quiet place, somewhere to daydream. A place to become lost in thought. So easy to forget the task that had been assigned to you. But the requirements of a small farm were constant. The need for water an ever-present task. No sooner was the bucket emptied but it was needed to be filled again and again and again. The track to the spring was as well worn as that of a pilgrim's path.

I often considered the construction of the well and tried to imagine the men who dug down into the guts of the world to find clean constant water. They lined the sides with dressed stone. My uncle warned me that it was bottomless. To prove his claim he had me cock an ear and listen when he dropped a pebble into the well. The small stone broke the meniscus surface and drove concentric ripples before it.

No matter how I cocked the shell of my ear, I could never hear the sound of that pebble reaching the distant bottom. I held my breath and tried to stop the clockwork spin of the world but it was of no use, the well held onto the secret of its dimensions.

My uncle was one of the first in the locality to sign up for the new electricity. There was a plug and a switch and a bulb and before long the notion that you could pump water directly to the house and yard using a submersible motor. The neighbours were having new wells sunk. It was the talk of the creamery yard and the church gate. No more dragging buckets from the well. No more stumbles through the nettles and docks of the back haggard, or ducking the low-hanging mossy branches of the crab trees in the old orchard. No more accidental splashes down the tops of wellington boots or wringing out the wet hem of my dress. Why would anyone think twice. It was as they might say nowadays – a no-brainer.

The dowser was summoned by my uncle but he had to be patient and wait. It seemed that the specialist's services were in high demand at this time. But one early summer's day he cycled into the yard. I can see him still in my mind's eye. A serious man with a crown of wavy hair that rose from his head as if he himself had been plugged into a live socket. He had what we schoolgirls cruelly and mockingly called 'Sam Maguire' ears. They stuck out from his head at right angles, not unlike the handles on that much-coveted All-Ireland football trophy.

There was a stained canvas bag tied to the carrier of his bicycle, and the dowser removed this and held it under his arm like a bagpipe as he walked about the farmyard beside my uncle. On that day, someone took a photograph of the man. I still have it. He wears a collarless shirt and braces to hold up his high-waisted trousers.

I see that the braces are attached to mis-matched buttons sewn onto the waistband of those self-same trousers. But the thing of interest in the photograph is the hazel fork that he holds in his upturned fists. When the camera shutter was engaged, it caught the dowsing tool parallel to the ground. There is a look of intense concentration on the diviner's face. Poised between heaven and earth, the miracle is yet to be performed.

The dowser found water in the yard, convenient to the cow house. A well was sunk and a tap spluttered and then gushed new water into a Belfast sink in the kitchen. There was an outside tap in the yard and soon creeping buttercup, vetch, mare's tails and a variety of hardy colonisers softened the path to the old well. I'd go there from time to time to dream and trail my fingers through the surface tension of the crystal water before scooping up and drinking back a palmful of cold sweetness.

My uncle knew I went there and voiced that he was mortally afraid that someone, I assumed he meant me, might one day accidentally stumble and fall down into those bottomless depths and be drowned.

He covered in the well with stone slabs and, just to be sure, a cap of thick concrete and that might have been the end of an era and a drift into the new modern age. – but it wasn't.

He could never quite forget the well. The tea made from water boiled from the kitchen tap, from the new well, he said never tasted the same. He'd sometimes tip his scalding tea into the saucer and, avoiding my Aunt's frown, slurp it and smack his lips. With a shake of his head he'd pronounce that there was never tea like the stuff wet with the water from the old well.

And who knows, perhaps he was right? Maybe that was yet another secret held in the 'bottomless' depths of the spring in the backfield, deep in the dark underbelly of the world.

Áine Nic Liam is a Dubliner who is a keen gardener, artist and world adventurer.

29

When Shay Lost Out To The ESB Lodger

Mary O'Connor

HE ran across the bog and through the gorse – a mass of yellow bloom with its glorious fragrance wafting on the breeze. He had the ferret in the sack and the two rabbits slung across a stick. Aunt Kate would make rabbit stew and later he would fry the leftovers in the pan on the open fire. Fried rabbit tasted great.

She was polishing the glass globe of the oil lamp with newspaper. Shay loved the way the lamp light cast shadows over the kitchen especially when the men came in to 'mitch.' 'I won't have to do this much longer' she said as he came in the door. 'I'm getting the electric, I signed up today. They're running a line near here and they said it won't take too long till I'll be all lit up. They say that thirty men will be working at it and some of them will be locals.'

Shay didn't like the idea of the light coming to Aunt Kate's. They had it at home in the town and his mother had a washing machine and a hoover and she was getting a fridge. He knew that Aunt Kate's with its whitewashed walls and big open fire would never be the same again. The magic of the oil lamp in his bedroom casting its shadows on the walls and the patchwork quilt and the way he could move his hands and fingers to project the heads of birds and wild animals would be gone forever.

He loved spending the school holidays with Aunt Kate who was a widow and who allowed him to 'rule the roost.' He went outside to look at the sunset, a flaming ball going down behind the fir trees way across the river. It was then he saw it running across the clais, an animal, a creature, a monster, he wasn't sure but he was definite that he had never seen the like before, as he watched it disappear through the gorse and the hazel bushes beyond. He knew it was an omen of some kind. He shivered.

Later, as Shay played a game of 25 with Aunt Kate there was a knock on the door. It was unusual, as it was way too early for the 'mitchers' who always lifted the latch and walked in.

He followed Aunt Kate to the door and saw a giant of a man in a brown striped suit, brown leather rubber soled shoes and a head of brown hair greased to the last with hair oil. He had a pair of hands like shovels and a hard red-skinned face.

Shay didn't like the look of him. "I hear you might keep a lodger," he said. Aunt Kate looked at him strangely.

"I'm working with the ESB. They're running a line along here. I'll be around here for a good while and I'm looking for somewhere to stay," the man added.

"Do you drink?" asked Aunt Kate. Shay knew she didn't like drink as the poteen that Uncle Benny made and hid in her bog had been the cause of his fall into the bog hole.

"Never touched it in me life ma'am, never broke me confirmation pledge," he retorted.

He knew that was it, Aunt Kate was going to take in Jack Kelly as a lodger. "I'll be wantin' a good dinner in the evening and plenty of ham and cheese sandwiches for me lunch box," Kelly went on.

"This your young fella?" he queried as he scowled at Shay "Me nephew. Out from the town on school holidays," Aunt Kate replied.

The next morning Shay was recruited to get the spare room with the fireplace ready for Kelly. New sheets made from flour bags were taken from the hot press beside the fire in the kitchen and blankets and an eiderdown were taken down. A white enamel basin with a blue rim and a jug to match were placed on the washstand and a bar of red carbolic soap alongside.

Two new red and white towels added to this display of grandeur and a mat recently purchased from Mrs. Kiely the travelling woman was placed on the floor beside the bed. Aunt Kate cleaned the window and hung the bright yellow curtains. He found a box of drawing pins and wondered if he should scatter a handful between the new sheets. Kelly was due to arrive that evening.

Shay was sent up to the high field to 'dig' the dinner. From the high field he could see across the bog towards the power station in Portarlington and he knew the new line where Kelly worked would get the power from there. He looked at the spade. It was sharp. You could hit a good skelp with it. He took a few practice swipes.

When he arrived at the house Aunt Kate was bringing a big piece of bacon from the dairy where she kept it in a cement tank with a big wooden lid. He washed the potatoes in the bucket with rainwater from the barrel and a stick. She peeled and sliced the turnips. A freshly baked cake of bread and a currant cake were cooling on the windowsill. He noticed she was wearing a new apron and her hair was tied back. The table with the oilcloth beside the window had three settings.

Shay heard Kelly's bicycle crunching the gravel. During the meal he told Aunt Kate that he worked with Matt Ryan's gang. They were putting up the poles. Matt stayed in lodgings in the town along with the other gangers. They got great grub and liked the odd jar. They went home at weekends as they all had cars. She seemed very interested and asked Kelly if he was ever married. He said no.

Shay was ignored. He went up to his room and he could hear Kelly and Aunt Kate talking for a long time.

She usually went to town on a Friday to do the shopping which she brought home in two hessian bags on the handlebars of the bike and she often brought a parcel on the carrier. "I'll be late home this evening," she told Shay. "You can boil the potatoes and cabbage for Jack and you can fry a few eggs. I'm getting me hair permed in McGiffes. Pauline is going to give me a 'Wella' that's the very latest."

Shay didn't like the sound of it and it looked as if Kelly was getting his feet under the table.

She arrived home with her hair curled and she looked different. She smiled at Kelly, waiting for him to comment. Shay ate his dinner in silence. Aunt Kate was changing, Kelly was the cause of it and he didn't like it. He went outside and stuck a nail into the back tyre of Kelly's bike. He heard herself and Kelly talk long into the night.

Kelly stayed over at the weekend and both he and Aunt Kate went cycling on Sunday afternoon. Shay thought they went towards Killeigh as Kelly said he had an uncle living there. He was in bed and the fire was out when they arrived home. He knew she would have to light it again to boil the kettle. He didn't make the sandwiches for Kelly's lunch.

The next day Aunt Kate went to the town again and Shay was told to 'put on' the dinner for Kelly, boiled bacon, cabbage and potatoes. "I'll bring you home a comic," she said. He wondered why she was going again so soon.

She arrived back with two huge bags, marked 'Lees of Portarlington' and handed him 'The Beano' and 'The Dandy.' She went to her bedroom with her purchases. "That's me weddin' suit and hat," she told Shay when she returned to the kitchen.

"Meself and Jack are getting married Wednesday week. It'll be great to have a man about the house again."

"But sure you have a man when you have me," said Shay. "Sure your only a gossoon," she said, "and anyway you'll be going home to your Ma on Saturday. Your father is collecting you in the car."

"But Ma said I'd be here until the end of August," he said. "That was before Jack," she said. "He only wants the two of us," she said firmly.

Aunt Kate was a stranger now. Kelly didn't like him and Kelly was going to marry her next week. He would never be invited out for holidays again.

He saw the two large bottles of Taylor-Keith's Lemon Soda on the dresser which Aunt Kate bought for Kelly in the village shop. Earlier that summer, he discovered where Uncle Benny had hidden the poteen in the bog and he dug up a bottle. He drank half the Lemon Soda from each bottle; then filled them with poteen and replaced the cap firmly.

Mary O'Connor is a PhD legal researcher at Queens University, Belfast and lives in Edenderry, Co Offaly. She is a well-known writer with a keen interest in literature and history.

30

Power Comes To Enniskerry In The 1920s

Brian White

WITH the arrival of a new Parish Priest, the Rev Thomas Waters in Enniskerry in 1924, the parishioners did not know what to expect when he proposed that they should form a Power Supply Co-Operative Society and harness the Glencullen River to generate their own electricity.

He wanted it to run on similar lines to Glencree Reformatory, Powerscourt and the Bray Electric Light Company. Lord Powerscourt became chairman of the new society, Rev Waters as president and Mary Wogan (Terry Wogan's aunt) as its secretary.

The society sold £5 share certificates to raise the capital to build the works on the Glencullen River at Knocksink. Within a few months they had sold 91 and the project was given the green light.

Local labour was used to build a dam on the river 60 feet wide and 15 feet high; they also built the power station and millrace 100 feet long. Messrs Green of Dublin electrical contractors fitted out 40 homes in readiness of the power station coming live in April 1925.

Homes could have one plug socket and maximum of three light switches. Lady Powerscourt performed the opening ceremony after which they adjourned to the Powerscourt Arms Hotel for dinner.

One of the first customers of the Enniskerry Electric Supply Co-Operative Society was Rathdown Rural No.2 Council who decided to erect six street lights in the village.

The sluice gates of the dam were opened every evening by Tom Arnold who also ran the forge in the village. This allowed the customers of the society to enjoy two hours of electricity. The immediate change was the use of the wireless from dry cell batteries to a steady supply of current.

By 1937, the society had 46 consumers and the tariff for lighting was one shilling per unit and four pence per unit to a power socket. The society sold in the year ending March 1936 a total of 6,258 units.

Next purchase of residents list was a vacuum cleaner and electric cookers. Lives of individuals in the village would change for ever, even playing card games late into the evening in the AOH Hall next door to the Wogan household.

In 1927, Mary Wogan's mother Sarah took ill and Lord Powerscourt's estate agent, Mr. Abraham Chatteron, wrote a letter to all the residents of Enniskerry appealing for them to be quiet after 10pm so Mrs Wogan could get some rest.

In 1947, the Enniskerry Electric Supply Co-Operative Society was acquired by the ESB and the change over from the local supply to the national grid for its 58 customers. That left Wicklow County Council with a building on the Glencullen River that was a danger to local children swimming in the river.

The following year the decision was taken to blow up the power-station. A police sergeant and a member of the county council was dispatched to Kilcock to get gelignite and on their return it was used to destroy the buildings and dam.

When the school children got their summer holidays the structure of the power station was gone. All that remains of the Enniskerry Electric Supply Co-Operative Society is a couple of share certificates and part of the dam wall in Knocksink wood.

Footnote: The Rev Waters left Enniskerry for Ballybrack Parish in County Dublin in 1926 and died seven months after leaving Enniskerry. Mary Tallon nee Wogan died in 1949.

Brian White is a writer and historian who lives in Bray Co. Wicklow.

31

A Lifetime Between Poles

Gerry Malone

IN October 1953 at the age of 29 my father Paddy Malone was one of five men hired on a temporary basis by the ESB area manager to work in the bringing of electricity to the village of Corofin, County Clare as part of the ESB Rural Electrification Scheme.

There were over 50 men from the locality available for work at the time, and he felt very fortunate to be one of those selected. Each employee had to supply his own shovel and when hired they reported to the local temporary ESB depot at "The Old School" in Corofin where they were provided with a pick and crowbar which they were to use in the digging of holes for the erection of poles in order to carry the ESB lines.

Work commenced at 8am at Ballykinacorra North, also known as 'The New Line,' which was a low-lying area prone to flooding a mile outside the village on the road from Corofin to Ennis. The initial line was pegged out where the poles were to be erected and all five men got a pegged area in which to dig a six-foot deep hole.

My father was fortunate in that in his allocated area he did not encounter rock or pools of water which some co-workers did. Consequently he was the first man to have dug the hole for the erection of the first pole to bring electricity to Corofin by early morning.

When it was time to erect each pole they were put in place manually by pulling it upright with ropes and the strategic placement of a tripod. My father was then asked by the foreman to fit the timber T-bar near the top of the pole that held the ESB lines in place. This needed to be done before erection. He became so adept at the job that thereafter he was no longer required to dig any more holes, and was given the job of T-bar fitter.

He later became involved with another man in the sledging of poles by pony in soft ground and inaccessible areas in the locality. At that time there was no mechanical assistance on site and all work was done manually.

After approximately eight months, with the completion of the local scheme he was asked to locate to the commencement of the scheme for the electrification of Tulla, a village about 20 miles from Corofin. He declined the offer, feeling it was too far to travel from his home. With hindsight he regretted turning down the opportunity as he felt he would have eventually been made permanent and his life would have been much easier.

In July 1997 – 44 years later – the ESB replaced the poles on 'The New Line' with taller ones and add coloured wire because swans were hitting the lines when landing and taking off in the flooded area in winter, causing energy outages.

My father was on hand, and in a sentimental moment, requested possession of the first pole for which he had dug the pole. The person in charge duly obliged.

That pole was later erected on my father's land by my brother Kevin who had inherited the farm, as a way of carrying a low voltage line for strip grazing land, on the other side of the road from the main farm buildings.

The pole remains in very good condition, and as a reminder to future generations Paddy felt that it was important to enlighten people of the history of the pole by commissioning and placing a plaque on the pole. It remains in situ to this day.

Patrick (Paddy) Malone (92) was born in Cragmoher, Corofin, County Clare and lived on the family farm. He married Maureen O'Connor from Kinvara, Co Galway in 1956 and they had five children. Gerry is his son.

32

Putting A Plan B In ESB

Christy King

I BEGAN working for the ESB on September 21, 1953, aged 19. One of my first jobs was stringing distribution lines along predefined routes to facilitate housing connections in what was then a very rural Carrigadrohid, in Co Cork.

One thing to remember about that time was that clothes were in short supply; you had your Sunday best and a separate set of working clothes if you were lucky.

As a part-time musician, I felt the pressure to dress well as it was a requirement of all band members to do so. I was very impressed by John Guinevan, with whom I would be working and later became great friends, as he was one of two well-dressed men in our group that day.

I assumed that he was an engineer and had been working at the job for many years but later found out that he was only wearing such sharp clothing because he had spent the weekend in Cork city and hadn't had a chance to change his clothes that morning.

We moved from house to house, connecting each one up to the system as we went along and I quickly realised that if you wanted to climb the ladder in the ESB, the top of the pole was the place to start.

Work was scarce at that time and it was important to look busy or else you could easily be replaced from one day to the next. Every time a supervisor came to visit, John had me working overhead, which paid off quickly. After a week John got promoted and I got his job. It was as we began to connect the houses on the main Macroom road that we began to run into a bit of resistance from the residents. Being local lads, we were known in the area and people wondered how we had acquired the necessary knowledge about electricity in such a short space of time. Their worries were put at bay when we explained that our work was being supervised on an hourly basis.

It was the parish priest's honour to perform the first official switch on, but with about 15 minutes to go before the allotted time, we realised that the switch was not connected to the power.

It fell to Con Shanahan to scale the transformer pole and to put the fuse in at the same time the priest pulled the switch – the light came on successfully and the town, including the priest, were left in the dark about who truly was the first person to illuminate their town.

As we travelled around, we'd stay in digs or sometimes even with family. At one stage I stayed with a very religious cousin of my mother's and felt as if I had landed in a house of prayer.

One Friday morning, as I prepared my usual breakfast fry of rashers and sausages before work, I heard her shout indignantly: "This is Friday. No meat, you should know that. Leave the meat for the cats." Naturally, I did what I was told and popped some rashers into the pan for the lucky cats, although not before enjoying my own fry up first.

The cats seemed content to conspire with me and Cousin Helen remained none the wiser, as I certainly never let the cat out of the bag.

Transportation was something that was severely lacking in the early days of the ESB, the use of the pony and trap, as well as the bicycle, continued into the 1950s, although supervisors began to use vans in the 1940s and trucks were also introduced to drop off and collect men from the site each day.

I earned a reputation as a good driver and spent much of my time after the late 1950s working behind the wheel of a tractor. Although I enjoyed this work, it went against me when I later applied for my first permanent job as a linesman in Fermoy. Good driver though I may have been, I had little use for a vehicle that was not fully functioning.

On one occasion I recall being asked by a supervisor to accompany a truck driver to Cork pole field to collect a tractor that required reconditioning and new tyres. The tractor wasn't ready when I arrived, giving me the opportunity to look around and admire a new tractor parked at the back of an empty shed. The thought crossed my mind to take it away and pretend that it was a mistake but after I started it up I realised that there was no compressor fitted.

After waiting quite a while, my machine eventually came along, complete with new tyres and little other improvement. Even the battery was flat! When I protested, the pole field supervisor gave me a lecture on budgeting and I even felt some sympathy for him...until plan B kicked in, that is.

Instead of driving home with my tail between my legs, I parked my tractor next to the new one and switched the batteries in no time at all. The unsuspecting field supervisor – probably glad to see the back of me – saluted with a wave of his hand as I drove off, which I returned wholeheartedly indeed.

Christy Ring began working with the ESB in 1953 and was appointed to the staff in 1961. An outstanding musician, he married in 1960 and has three children. His autobiography, 'Tales from Fermoy' was published in 2007.

"A few houses in our parish were the last of the great rural electrification round up. One might as well try to pull teeth with a tweezers as get money out of some of them to pay for the transformer."

Monica Weir – 'Sir, I've No Homework Because The New Light Blinded Me'

33

'Sir, I've No Homework Because The New Light Blinded Me'

Monica Weir

AH, I remember it well – the huge shadows, the spooky corners, the flicker of candles, and the paraffin lamplight. The scent it gave off mingled with the smell of the turf fire will remain a treasured memory forever.

Searching underneath the bed and in the wardrobe for ghosts before getting into bed for the night came to an abrupt end in the early sixties with the onset of rural electrification for households like ours.

A few houses in our parish were the last of the great rural electrification round up. One might as well try to pull teeth with a tweezers as get money out of some of them to pay for the transformer.

Eventually my father paid for it all with my mother saying: "May the divil pull it out of them."

The local handyman wired our house; it seemed to take an eternity. We would hold the white plastic conduits as he slowly threaded the wires through. The little round piece of timber attached to the walls held the sockets for the lights and plugs. It looked very ornate.

At last the day for getting connected to the main supply arrived. I was first to switch on the light in our house. The excitement was surreal, it was like a Christmas morning.

The children raced up and down the stairs, nearly knocking each down in the mad rush to be first to turn on the light.

"Miracles will never cease," said my mother adding that she would leave the oil lamp hanging for some time yet just in case.

And how right she was. High winds and falling trees brought the wires down and would have left us in the dark only for the old reliable oil lamps.

In school the day after we got the light the teacher asked my brother why he had not done his lessons. He could scarcely reply as he was filled with pride and excitement.

Finally he blurted out: "Sir, I couldn't do my homework because the new light blinded me."

The teacher smiled as she looked at him saying: "I heard many an excuse in my time but that one beats Banagher."

Monica Weir hails from Roscommon and has 12 fabulous grandchildren living nearby. She enjoys writing short stories and childrens stories as one of her many hobbies.

34

The Power Of Gentle Persuasion

Mark McGaugh

IN the sleepy hamlet of Glassvalley, a picturesque village which nestles cosily on the shore of Lough Corrib in County Mayo, the Varley family, whom hitherto were the hallmark of democracy in the local community, were seriously divided on the question of electricity both in the community and in their own home.

The two unmarried brothers Peter and Pat, lived with their spinster sisters in a neatly kept thatched cottage, with sweet smelling roses forming an archway on the sanded pathway to the front door. Peter, the eldest in the family, was normally considered by his brother and sisters to be spokesperson on important issues.

Therein lay the conundrum for Peter, because he was partly in agreement with his brother Pat that they would not have the electricity in the house, while in the interest of domestic bliss and a good understanding, he was forced to listen and heed their two sisters who were convinced that there were many advantages in having the electric light installed.

Mary and Nora had visited a store in Galway where they saw an electric iron, electric cookers, even fridges where they could store the milk and to crown it all they saw an electric radio. It so happened that Peter ant Pat were ardent radio listeners and while Pat was mounting his anti-electric crusade he was careful not to mention to anyone in the house or in his local, the Headford Arms pub, that one of his considerations for having the electric installed would be the benefit of the electric radio.

He reminded himself of the recent incident when he was cycling home from town and the acid spilled on his best Sunday trousers.

Except that tailor Quincy had advised him to have the second pair of trousers made for a few shillings extra when he had the suit made 10 years earlier, Pat would have been in a right state without his best trousers.

Much depended on the meeting which he and Peter had planned to attend in the local community hall. Peter decided that when their opportunity arose Pat would be their spokesperson. The hall was packed with the panel of electricity experts on the stand ready to answer all the serious technical questions likely to arise.

John Murphy wanted answers to "how he was going to be compensated" for the poles which would stretch across his land as he had been reliably informed in the pub that hardly any grass was ever likely to grow again in the fields where the poles were erected.

Mike Toher though was all in favour because the electric milking machine would help him enormously with his dairy herd.

Pat Varley could hardly control his increasing annoyance when he caught the eye of the chairman. He stood up, asking them "if they had all taken leave of their senses."

Who was going to attach electric connectors from the milking machine to cows udders? He certainly was not because his two sisters had milked their cows for the last 20 years and they were not going to risk their four shorthorn cows to be damaged forever.

Who'd want electric lights in every room anyway when they had bought enough candles on Candlemas day to last for years? Pat continued to lay the strongest possible objections to every argument put by those in favour of electricity.

Peter was very impressed by Pat's performance but he always knew that his brother was capable of great things. He recalled the time when Pat nearly emigrated. He made it as far as Galway station but missed the train to Dublin because he had a few drinks at the Great Southern Hotel. The following morning at breakfast he decided that London was not for him and Peter and the two sisters welcomed home the prodigal son with open arms.

It did not matter to the brothers that the vote was overwhelmingly in favour for electricity. They were more concerned at what their sisters would think of them for voting against the proposal.

They showed their discontent when they had to iron the shirts and the trousers on Saturday nights. They also made comments about the danger of the Tilley lamp in the sheds and near the hay barn.

They hinted as time went on that they had no interest in having an electric fire, which gave the turf fire a stay of execution and welcome news to Pat and Peter.

Their strip of bog in Dalgan had produced the best possible quality black turf over the years, and although they admitted to the work being back-breaking and tough, it was a lot better heat than any electric fire was likely to produce.

The real doubt though in the minds of the brothers came when their Dublin cousin extolled the virtue of the electric radio.

Pat listened to the old style battery operated radio, morning, noon and night. He would listen to the 'Kennedy's of Castleross, the Donnelly's Sausage's programme, but above all else his ear was glued to the radio on Sunday afternoons when the golden voice of Michael O'Hehir gave the glorious commentaries on the football and hurling matches.

He was an ardent GAA fan especially of his native county Mayo who were at that time the All Ireland champions. Mayo had proudly taken Sam across the Shannon in 1950, and again in 1951. Pat thought it would be a mighty event to have the electric radio installed in time for the next All Ireland final to hear the voice of Michael O'Hehir.

The sisters saw Pat weakening and left an advert for the latest electric Philips radio on the breakfast table the following morning while a further advert for the latest electric iron was strategically positioned nearby. This was the final powerful persuasion that Pat fell for, as the description in the advert captivated his desire and finally removed his objections to the installation of electricity.

When the community organised a party which took place several weeks later to celebrate the 'switch on,' Pat, who had voted against it a short time before, now took pride of place in the middle of the floor describing how he could now listen to programmes on sport and politics and farming from all over the world. He said there was even a programme telling him what the weather forecast was likely to be in the coming days.

Jokingly he told anyone who'd listen that even the crease in his trousers was better since they brought the new electric iron into the house.

Mark McGaugh is a native of Shrule, Co Mayo but now lives in England. Married with three grown-up children and five grandchildren, the retired businessman enjoys writing as a pastime.

35

The Christmas Puddings' Surprise

Anna Jacob Tolan

IT was late November in 1953 and I was 10 when the 'switch on' in our house took place. Before that, we were fortunate in that we had gas light in the main areas of the house and the old reliable oil lamps for the bedrooms.

My evening job was to "do the oils" – fill the lamps and bottles for the oil heaters, thus exonerating me from wash-up duties as I might have oil on my hands.

My father decided some months earlier to have the house wired through the gas fittings in the attic and we had pull-cord switches suspended from the ceiling in the 'front' rooms.

He did not like to see the conduit on the wall with the big black switch. This was alright for the kitchen, hallway and other areas. There was one outlet socket in some rooms, and one in the kitchen, and these were discreetly wired down the wall, usually hidden in a corner.

For a few weeks before the switch on, my father bought a washing machine, a Burco boiler, an iron and a kettle.

On the evening of the switch on we had a demonstration on how to use the washing machine. The Burco boiler was there to heat the water for it but he also came up with a greater use for the same boiler.

He loved Christmas pudding and my mother would make plenty for him in boiled sweet-cans. These had tight fitting lids and were used extensively for that purpose.

She would make the puddings and he would take care of the water levels during the boiling process.

This entailed several big pots with boiling water on top of the range.

The pots had to be topped up and rotated regularly during an evening.

The electric Burco boiler took care of all this in one go holding three cans at one time. He was like a child with a new toy... and there was a Christmas theme to it.

Anna Jacob Tolan is from Knockanillaun, Ballina, but now resides in Crossmolina, Co Mayo. Retired with eleven grandchildren, she enjoys baking and embroidery.

36

Lighting On The Wall

Declan P. Gowran

A S dusk descended a spooky shadow blanket crept across the countryside, melting the landscape into darkened monochrome. The invading night stepped across the threshold of Carrigeen Cottage.

Inside Ned Carroll prepared the oil lamps. He delicately removed the bulbous glass covers and lit the wicks after trimming them as necessary. The lamps were used by purpose: a large one for the kitchen table and a smaller one for the mantelpiece. There were others too, designed to be carried; but we were forbidden to hold them for fear of burning ourselves or inadvertently causing a fire by dropping them.

Ned allowed my big brother Jimmy and me to operate the wick wheel under his supervision. As we manipulated the intensity of the lamplight, spectral shadows danced across the walls and ceiling. A heat haze shimmered above the funnel of the glass cover, and the smell of the paraffin oil was like medicine. Its burnt incense made me sleepy.

Ned handled the Sacred Heart lamp with special reverence. Unlike the other lamps with the clear glass globed reflectors and tin metal oil well with wick adjustment wheel, the Holy Lamp as he called it, had a red reflector and a brass body to afford it more elegance. Ned placed it, flickering deep red, on the small wooden shelf beneath the brass framed picture of the Sacred Heart that hung on the mantelpiece above the fireplace. As if to complement it Cathleen Carroll, Ned's wife, had placed two other pictures either side of it: these depicted bucolic scenes.

With the glowing of the lamps illuminating the kitchen we gathered around the fire in the great kitchen hearth. Tom Byrne would sit in the seat formed by the partition of the doorway and fill a dudeen with tobacco. He told stories about 'Black Bran', Bran Dubh Mac Echach, an ancient warrior from West Wicklow whose exploits are recorded in the Annals of Ulster or Michael Dwyer in that slurping voice of his. He always took his supper with the Carrolls before heading home. Ned would pare a twist of plug tobacco for his briar pipe and recall his luck (or lack of luck) at the Saturday night 25s card game with the Card School in Irongrange.

Cathleen did her darning or knitting while planning the week's chores. So we listened before our copious yawns beckoned us to bed. Cathleen led the way with her oil-lamp and tucked us in. Before we closed our eyes we watched as her figure and the lamp were silhouetted against the wall as she descended the stairs slowly, leaving our bedroom in darkness. A whitewashed lighting on the wall caught the hushed voices downstairs as we drifted off to sleep.

Carrigeen Cottage seemed always cosy because the fire never went out. First thing in the morning Cathleen rekindled the flame by throwing on a log or two to spark it back to life. The expansive fireplace stood to the left as you entered the kitchen from the compact hall lobby. Behind the hallway partition Tom Byrne's throne was situated conveniently out of the draught of the hall door.

The hearth was stained a tarry black and was festooned with an array of crane-like hooks of various shapes and lengths. These hooks were used to swing the pots and pans back and forth over the heat of the flames. On the first night of our arrival a tar encrusted iron kettle hung, whistling to the boil ready to make the tea.

An equally tar encrusted skillet pot stood to the side of the range on an ingle-nook seat heaped with steaming potatoes. The ingle-nook seats were to become our favourite perches when listening to the stories in the cottage. Our weekly scrub taken in the zinc bath filled with hot soapy water in front of the fire.

Cathleen baked the best homemade bread ever on her range. It was like Manna from heaven, and tasted like it too. Her secrets were in her head: in the mixing of the correct amount of ingredients, the kneading of the dough: turning over and over as she hummed away. She used basic equipment: an enamel mixing bowl, milled flour or wholemeal, Baking Powder, cool spring water from the Pike, and buttermilk as necessary. The proportion of ingredients she knew instinctively. She would mix the ingredients in the basin on the sturdy kitchen table, chatting away as she did so, purely mechanical, kneading the dough over and over with her hands and fists.

She seemed to play with the lump of dough: bashing it, beating it, punching it, moulding it and fashioning it before flattening it. The shapely dough was then placed into the flat pan with the lid on and levered over the fire for baking. On top of the lid she would place hot pieces of logs lifted from the fire with the tongs so that the heat could radiate from above. In effect, the pan had taken on the aspect of an oven.

The woman knew intuitively when the bread was baked and all this done without fancy equipment bar a sieve. Yet the consistency was always right whether she baked wholemeal brown, soda bread or fruit cake. When she lifted the bread from the pan she always tapped the loaf on the bottom to make sure it was fully baked. Her bread was gorgeous, particularly when eaten hot with butter and maybe homemade jam dripping down the edges.

That's how it was when Jimmy and me first went to Carrigeen Cottage for our summer holidays.

Then one year when we arrived an energetic revolution had taken place. Electricity had arrived in Carrigeen cottage. The great range was still there for the fire; but now Cathleen cooked on an electric cooker just like those common in the city. She still baked her bread. But now the process was more efficient.

Times and temperatures could now be inputted into the oven guaranteeing consistent success. She could also use appliances like a food blender to diversify into cake baking or soup mixing. Aluminium took over as the main metal of pots and pans for home cooking. The iron pots could still be used to boil the spuds to feed the pigs that Ned Carroll raised for Christmas.

The biggest change of all was in the cottage lighting. Now she just flicked a switch to cast a powerful incandescent light across every room of the cottage. The electric light was much brighter and safer than the old lamp-light – if a little less romantic. They did not have to carry an oil-lamp to guide us upstairs to our bedroom.

And when she switched off our light before sleep the familiar voices and the lighting on the wall from the kitchen, reflected the spindles of the bannisters as if to reassure the two of us as we drifted off to sleep in this new era.

Only one thing in the cottage remained unaltered and unchanged: the red oil-lamp still glowed faithfully below the picture of the Sacred Heart above the mantelpiece of the kitchen.

Declan P Gowran is a retired driver and tour guide with Dublin bus. Married with four children and two grandchildren, he enjoys gardening and writing.

37

The Donegal Coasters

Des Doherty

A MAJOR difficulty in building rural networks was to get poles and other materials to remote locations. During the years of the Rural Electrification programme, well over one million wood poles had to be imported – mainly Sitka spruce – from Finland and Sweden, as well as two ship loads from Canada. A typical load was 10,000 poles. They were then conveyed from Dublin or Cork or Limerick by road or rail to the 800 plus Rural Areas around the Republic.

But bringing poles and heavy materials to Donegal posed special problems as the roads were – and are still – inadequate for heavy-duty road haulage. In addition there were very poor rail facilities, narrow gauge as well as wide gauge, and then there was the problem of cross border transport, with double and maybe triple unloading making the cost prohibitive.

A brave decision was made by ESB to send the pole cargoes to a number of West coast harbours and, in particular, to send virtually all Donegal supplies to local piers. They were ferried there by Dutch coasters: manned mainly by Dutch captains of whom it was often said: "They would go in anywhere" and some of whom already had experience with bulk pole shipments in the Baltic.

These skippers were now faced with the challenge of navigating into small harbours in West Donegal and Inishowen known as 'closed piers'. They were closed, in that they were to be used by fishermen only, but were soon going to become the drop off centres for delivering poles – up to the equivalent of 20 truck loads per coaster – directly to the isolated rural areas which required them.

The fact that they were closed piers also meant that no coasters or significant cargoes had ever come in there before which obviously increased the risks of the planned operation. In some cases special permission had to be granted by the Department of Industry and Commerce and also by the Revenue Commissioners.

Along the 400 miles of Donegal coastline, pole deliveries were made to: Malin Head, Moville, Culdaff, Letterkenny, Ramelton, Portsalon, Downings, Ards, Bunbeg, Burtonport, Teelin and Donegal Pier.

The first delivery was made in October 1953 to Ramelton where 500 locals turned out to cheer the Dutch Captain's seamanship and the heroics of the local unloaders: not to mention the "Christmas presents of electric light and power, and the comfort and prosperity that goes with them," for the people of Ramelton and Rathmullan."

It was virtually impossible to imagine the 8,800 of heavyweight poles required from 1954 to 1958 for the 9 Rural Areas of Inishowen being delivered other than by sea. Buncrana pier could take general material deliveries but around the peninsula, three piers were designated for pole deliveries: Moville; Bunagee Pier, Culdaff and Portmore Pier, Malin Head. In the latter case, older locals still remember the extraordinary sight of huge 'steamers' dwarfing the pier on two occasions to deliver up to 2,000 creosoted poles for Inishowen.

The first steamer was the famous MV Whitsun, skippered by Captain Jansen, which made a delivery in the spring of 1956 (958 poles destined for Clonmany Rural Area). Mary McLaughlin (S)* remembers the steamer being unloaded at high tide onto the nose of the pier, using her own cranes and slings.

As there wasn't enough space on the pier, the heavily creosoted poles were then carried by local men to a crisscrossed pole dump at the Pier Road. Capt. Jansen normally travelled with his family, and Philip Glackin was particularly impressed with the good-sized coal fire for cooking on board the coaster.

In February 1957, MV Ursa Minor made a second delivery of poles plus assorted materials from Limerick to Portmore Pier: This time for local use in Malin Rural Area. This coaster was brand new, having been commissioned in Groningen the previous year.

The Rural Engineer for Inishowen was Pat Quinn and his report marvelled at her dramatic struggle with the pier and the elements: "The ship's captain, finding no pilot available, elected to navigate the treacherous approaches unaided, and brought his ship safely alongside the pier. While some local 'salts' questioned his wisdom in so doing, there was no one to question his undoubted ability...."

Peter Conroy of ESB HQ also highlighted this delivery in his official report on the 'Donegal Coasters': "At Malin Head pier, the ship was eventually unloaded after continued dodging in and out of the single berth, to avoid the worst effects of a wrong-way wind which caused a dangerous under-surface ground swell".

When it is considered that the MV Ursa Minor was 46m long, while the old pier was only 90m (from the quay port to the nose) with a mere 20/30m effectively available for berthing, it shows how good the seamanship was and how hazardous the unloading.

From the pole dump above the pier, the materials were delivered by ESB lorries around the parish. But the delivery to work sites was not mechanised, and Annie Hunter remembers well the giant of a man with his piebald black and white pony who dragged individual poles across the fields of Ballyhillion. This was Jack Caulderbanks who lived in a Traveller's caravan with Penny, his remarkable pony. She was famous for 'slyping' the poles around obstacles to their final destination, usually near a sheough.

Their role was critical to the Rural Electrification programme, and their combined contract pay was 35 shillings a day. Jack unfortunately died in the 1960s in an accident near Glengad, but his son Paddy worked for ESB for many years, and Penny lived until a 'big age' too.

Later in that year, MV Whitsun got stranded in Bunagee harbour when Capt. Jansen ignored advice to divert his full load to Moville as a heavy swell was forecast. Without taking on a pilot, he managed to beach her on the quay port but with the coaster's stern stuck on a stag of rock (since removed) and her bow on the sand. While waiting for repairs and a high tide, the family stayed in Culdaff and the children went to school.

Local lore as recounted by Des Mills, and also Mickey (Denis Charlie) McDaid who worked on unloading the Whitsun, revelled in the contrast in cultures. In particular, local parents were very impressed with Dutch parental discipline: a slight tweak on the nose of a 'wain' was enough to stop all crying and bad behaviour.

And later again, the MV Whitsun, formerly named the Baltic was 'in the wars' as reported by Patsy Jordan of Malin, one of the ESB Rural Pioneers, when she was beached onto Arranmore Island in a gale. The family had to be rescued by the lifeboat, and the RNLI wanted to treat the MV Whitsun as salvage...ach sin scéal eile, mar a deirtear!

Safety of ESB personnel was, as always, very important. It is easy to understand that unloading had to be very rapid because it was dangerous to miss a tide, and fishermen had to be allowed get back to operations as quickly as possible. The unloaded cargo was then brought quickly to local pole dumps near the pier. One fatal accident was recorded in that context: in August '57 at a pole dump near Culdaff.

As a crew was unloading a load of poles (which the MV Whitsun had delivered to Bunagee) a Clonmany man, Dan McEleney, was struck by one of the poles. The injured man was brought to Carndonagh hospital and later died there. The report of the coroner, Dr Friel, concluded that it was: "An unfortunate accident...no blame could be attached to any one."

There was a special problem with the creosote or tar that was used to protect the poles against rot. It could cause discomfort to people when they had to carry poles (which were also very heavy) on their shoulders. Former "Rural Pioneers" still talk about the stinging in their ears as the strongest negative memory they have of trying to unload the steamers.

As a footnote, the head of ESB transport operations was Peter Conroy. He organised the whole fleet of coasters and became, as Michael Shiel refers to him in his book, 'The Quiet Revolution,' a 'Commodore' of ESB's rural organisation fleet.

The Donegal Coasters became indispensable on at least one occasion. In the spring of 1958, poles were urgently required so that the Drung Rural Area could be finished on time. While nearby Moville's "famine pier" had already taken deliveries from the MVs

Tura, Truus and Port Talbot over 1955/56, those poles were mainly for erection throughout Inishowen.

There had been very heavy snowfalls in the new year of '58 and for six weeks, apparently, Inishowen roads were inaccessible to practically all road transport.

In these circumstances it was of tremendous benefit that a steamer, the MV Andromeda, was able to dock at Moville pier and deliver the required poles and drums of conductor to Drung locations near the town. This time, to quote from Pat Quinn's report: "The 'undependable' sea was a winner."

Denotes a member of a certain family.

Des Doherty is a Donegal man who worked as a manager for ESB. He has written and lectured extensively on Rural Electrification, particularly relating to the Inishowen Peninsula.

"The poles were a nuisance in a field of wheat. There were rumours that cattle liked to use them or their stay wires as scratching posts and could get electrocuted."

**Denis Leonard –
'Assault On The Battery'**

38

Assault On The Battery

Denis Leonard

THE Shannon Scheme was coming. Well, it had been coming for 25 years or more.

At that time, the ESB was spreading distribution lines around rural areas providing much needed power to country houses and farms. We were in Meath, only 20 miles outside Dublin and it still had not reached us. Now, in early 1950s, they were actually asking our permission to erect a line of poles across our fields. That was probably just a formality as we stood little chance of stopping them, even if we wanted to be obstructive.

The poles were a nuisance in a field of wheat. There were rumours that cattle liked to use them or their stay wires as scratching posts and could get electrocuted.

The high voltage lines would pass close to our farmyard. Now we had a hectic scramble to get the yard, and some farm workers' cottages wired up in time to pass inspection by the ESB for connection as soon as possible.

I knew enough about electricity to do the work.

All I needed was some advice as to the size of the rubber-insulated cables to be used for the essential lighting and power points indoor and weatherproof fittings outdoors.

The benefits to the farm would be considerable. We could have a large fan heater under a porous floor in the barn for drying grain.

I could use an electric drill and other power tools in the workshop.

Lights all around made it easier to continue working after the early dusk in winter. Best of all, we now could use electric shears, much faster and easier for shearing our flock of sheep.

There was one potentially serious mistake. One of our farm workers complained that his new electric kettle gave him a shock.

The cottage wiring had passed inspection only the previous week, so I was confident we had done nothing wrong. I checked the fuse. It had blown.

I took out the fuse holder and touched the appliance with a new phase tester. The frame was still live. Going back to the fuse board, I found the ESB had connected their red incoming line to the neutral bar, the black to what should be the fuse protected live side.

To make matters worse, the technicians who came the next day to rectify the mistake somehow managed to drive their van to hit the gatepost and knocked it down. They had to pay to have it rebuilt.

Power sockets were of the two-pin side-earth type still used in Europe. Unlike the three-pin plugs we now use in British Isles, a plug could be inserted two ways, so you would not know which of the wires in the plug was live or neutral.

The big house was different.

Thirty years earlier, my grandfather had installed electric lights in the house, supplied from a large battery of 55 lead/acid cells on two racks behind a glass partition in a basement room. These charged up to 110 volts weekly as required from a generator driven by a single cylinder paraffin engine.

Edward, the gardener had charge of the system. He showed me the routine. We would test the acid density using a floating measure in a tube with a rubber suction bulb on top. Then we had to top up the batteries with distilled water taken from a large carboy brought from the chemist in Dunshaughlin.

Starting the engine was quite a process.

First, two brass cups were topped up with oil to drip slowly onto the crankshaft bearings. A similar cup would take a small amount of scarce petrol to drip into the cylinder. In the absence of petrol, a small amount of carefully warmed up paraffin might work.

A small lever would lift the exhaust valve so that a crank handle could freely turn the engine over fast enough for the two big flywheels to complete a compression stroke.

Electric Dream:
A woman and her
children admire
an electric kettle
during an exhibition
in May, 1954.

**The First
Electric Car!** An
ESB van in rural
Ireland in the 1940s.

*Photographs Courtesy
ESB Archives*

Power To The People: A 1950s exhibition showcasing the many practical uses for electricity on the farm.

Tap Man: James Dillon at the ICA Fair in 1950. The banner behind him reads, 'Don't carry water to your home... Make it run'.

Running Water: A giant tap is exhibited at the Cork Show in 1960.

Pump It Up: An ESB information pamphlet points out the numerous benefits of having pumped water in your home.

Taking The Plunge: A farmer decides to have a pump installed on his farm in the 1950s.

The Big 'Switch On': CS Andrews, Seán Lemass, E Enwright and R F Browne at Ballinamult in Co Waterford.

Big Changes: A young mother and her children in the 1950s.

Showcase: An ESB employee shows off the latest electric gadgets.

Electric Goods: A sales van visits a family in rural Ireland in 1956.

Roll Up, Roll Up... An ESB promo poster for a
demonstration of farm and domestic appliances.

**Beauty For
The Beast:**
A whitehead
cow gets
an electric
grooming at a
demonstration
in 1964 as
bemused
farmers
watch on.

Where Old Meets New: Old and new Ireland collide at an outdoor demonstration in July 1957.

At Your Service: Pamphlets promoting the benefits of hooking up to electricity.

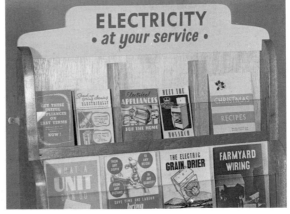

Sparks Fly: A welder gets the full benefit of electricity in his rural workshop.

Churning It Out: Hygiene and cooling of milk improves as electricity gets to the dairy door.

Food For Thought: A 1950s cookery demonstration.

Say Cheese: Smiling staff demonstrating in Navan, Co Meath in the 1960s.

Offloading: Poles arrive from Finland to be distributed around the country in the 1950s. *Photograph courtesy: Miranda Conroy*

Hot Water: A 1959 display promotes the simple joys of electricity.

Flour Power: A 1960 breadbaking demonstration.

All Mod Cons: A modern living exhibition in May 1960.

Numbers Game: ESB van proudly shows off how many households have signed up to the Rural Electrification Scheme.

Ready, Steady, Dough: Participants poised to begin at the National Breadbaking Championship of 1966.

Then close the exhaust valve, turn on the paraffin and hope it went, 'dunk-adunk-adunk'.

On the wall a large slate panel held knife switches and meter dials showing the voltage and current to charge the batteries.

When battery charging finished, the generator also powered a motor to pump water from our well up to the large storage tank high in the house.

During the 'emergency' years, paraffin was difficult to get, so we didn't use the lights very much, with candles or gas lamps instead. We then pumped the water by hand giving plenty of muscle building exercise to any of the grandsons willing to put in an hour or two of hard work.

Our first refrigerator worked by burning paraffin.

The approaching line of poles carrying the power supplies was very welcome. The big batteries were really at the end of their useful service. They would be very expensive to replace.

The old engine was redundant. So too was the motor to drive the water pump. A much smaller 'Stuart Centrifugal' pump, about the size of your hand replaced it. It worked automatically whenever the water level in the tank fell below a set mark.

A similar pump in the stable yard would provide water supplies to each of the horses in the yard.

A scrap merchant cast his eye over a large amount of good scrap iron and steel, and large bronze crankshaft bearings. He would dismantle it all and take it away in a van. All was well as he began to disconnect copper fuel pipes etc..

The big parts would be too heavy to lift out, so he decided to remove the large flywheels at each end of the crankshaft.

In my lessons about forge work, I had made a special tool for removing woodruff keys, the tapered wedge that fitted into a groove between the crankshaft and the big flywheels. That worked. But, the flywheels had been there for over 30 years and now refused to come off. The crank would still be too heavy to lift.

He went for his sledgehammer. Cast iron could be broken up. He was a big strong man and took a mighty swing with the hammer. The flywheel rang like a church bell. The head of the hammer flew off, crashed through the glass window of the battery room and just missed falling into or breaking one of the glass battery cells. The merchant let out a yell and ran off down the back lane ringing his hands. Ten minutes later, he got in his van and drove away. As far as I know, the old engine may still be there.

Later in my career, I would learn much more about generation and distribution of power. I would be in charge of four power plants, each one of which could supply a whole village. Yet, in my retirement, I am forbidden by law to do so much as instal a light or move a power socket in my own house. And that is progress.

Denis Leonard was born in Meath into a farming family. He learnt to fly aircraft from Weston Aerodrome and became a commercial pilot. He has been actively involved in representing many aspects of the airline industry.

39

Pulling The Wool Over Their Eyes

Tony McCormack

I T'S many years ago now since I stopped into a pub in the West of Ireland for lunch one day. There were two men in their early sixties sitting at the corner of the bar. They had been there a while... judging by the amount of empty glasses in front of them.

They put chat on me, possibly because they were after running out of something to say to each other. After talking to death the usual old faithfuls of the weather, GAA and politics, they asked me why I was in their part of the country.

I explained that I was an agricultural/veterinary rep calling to farmers in the region. They looked at each other and laughed. Then, after a small discussion between them, they shared a story with me, one that was 30 years old by then.

They were in the local pub having a few pints as younger men when a salesman called in and sat in roughly the same spot that I was sitting in. They obviously had a permanent residency at the bar.

They chatted to the stranger, probably for the same reason they were talking to me. He said he was in the area selling new electrical goods to farmers. At the time there was a revolution of new electrical machinery that would help to bring all farmers into the twentieth century.

It mainly consisted of companies importing equipment from the UK to sell here. He did his sales pitch. He was selling goods like skulling irons, shearing equipment, saws and drills. He enquired as to whether they would know of any potential customers.

The "devilment" was in the lads after a few pints so they sent him to a renowned local farmer, now long deceased. The farmer was at this stage in his early sixties. He was well-known for minding his money and every penny was a prisoner. According to the two lads, he could represent Connacht, never mind Leitrim in a meanness competition.

However, despite this drawback he was still well-liked and was seen as a pillar of the community and a great neighbour.

They persuaded the rep to navigate his car up the remotest of mountains on the promise that this man would buy an electric sheep shears. The lads were convinced that they had sent the unfortunate, gullible sales rep on a total dead rubber.

That evening the lads were still in the pub and a bit worse for wear when in came the farmer for his weekly drink.

The same pair used to hand-shear his sheep for him and it was the time of year for a deal to be done on the forthcoming job. Hand-shearing was a laborious, hard job that was dreaded by every sheep farmer. However, it had to be done in May/June as the wool provided the farmers with a substantial income.

The lads asked the farmer if he had purchased? To their surprise he cautiously said that he had, adding that the shearing would be a much easier job from now on. He threw in a curved ball by saying he would be looking for a generous discount on their cost of shearing per ewe.

They decided to give him a discount of roughly half the cost seeing as it should only take half the time to do the job. The lads shook on the deal and everyone resumed their socialising.

The following Monday they arrived up with their dogs to gather the sheep. The forecast was good for the following couple of days. The sheep were spread out over 1,000 acres of mountainous land known as commonage. All the farmers in the locality had their own farms and they also had grazing rights on this land.

In this case there were five others whose sheep were on the commonages with this farmer's sheep. They would all come together to gather the sheep for such jobs as dosing, weaning and shearing. They had 600 sheep between them.

All six farmers headed off in different directions, and two hours later they all had closed in on the sheep and with the 1,000 acres swept, they descended down the hill with their flocks.

The sheep all entered a large compound that in turn tapered them into a five-bay hayshed. This was the scene of many a backbreaking job in the past and would be the lads' home for the next few days. Or so they thought.

The sight of the shed brought many an unhappy memory for the lads. The only ray of light was the sight of the new poles and wire leading to the shed that in their eyes heralded a new era of sheep-shearing.

After changing their clothes to more suitable shearing attire, the lads approached the shearing pen to be greeted by the six men smirking and joking. The tight farmer turned to my two new friends and handed them two bright shiny hand-shears.

They said they nearly passed out when he told them that his new purchase was a brand new electrical sharpening stone.

This implement was indeed a help as it would replace the necessity to hand-sharpen the shears but it was far from the electric shears that they were dreaming about. The prospect of the upcoming hard slog sent them into despair especially as they had agreed to do it for half price. The farmer who had hoodwinked them turned to his neighbours and gave them another form of wink. The two drinking buddies had no choice but to grin and bear it.

Months later when they were back in their usual haunt keeping the bar propped up the same sales rep came back into the bar. He greeted them and they chatted politely before moving onto his sales escapades. He thanked them for their lead and offered to pay for a round of drink as a form of commission.

He recounted his deliberations with the farmer to them. He disclosed that he was about to shake on the sale of the electric shears when the other man asked him how he ended up arriving at his door.

The salesman told the farmer that he had been directed by the two lads in the pub that afternoon.

All of a sudden the sale was off. He just about managed to sell him the much cheaper sharpening stone.

He asked the farmer why he wouldn't save himself a lot of the backbreaking work. He said he knew the lads were trying to pull a stroke and he had an idea of how to get the last laugh – and make a saving at their expense.

Having won that battle, the farmer purchased the new shearing machine the following year that meant five days work was finished in two.

The two lads retained their position as chief shearers until the farmer passed on six years later. During that time and for many years after that, my two new friends had to suck up the fact that they were the butt of many a joke for being outwitted by the old man.

Tony McCormack is from Delvin, Co Westmeath. Married with two children, he is a development officer with Westmeath Community Development and enjoys writing as a hobby.

40

Power To The Islands
Mick Grealish

I WAS involved in the electrification on the Aran Islands, Omey Island and Inishboffin in the 1970s. I worked for the ESB as a charge hand linesman and engineering officer for over 40 years.

One day in 1973 I was called into the office at work and was told I was needed out in Inis Oir to build networks. There was a crew of six from Galway (including Jimmy Glynn and Jack Forde RIP) and we were told it involved 'one day's work'.

I headed off with one shirt and one pair of jeans. We spent three and a half hours on a small trawler and landed on the island. The following day we got the job done but no boat arrived back for two weeks. There were no planes on the island at the time. So I arrived back home into the Docks in Galway after doing one day's work in a fortnight because of the island weather.

Ruairi Siopa (Conneely) was the man who provided us with clothes, food and money. Ruairi would always say to us: "Don't be short." The money ran out but we were never short... for a pint of Guinness. We would go for our pint at night and on occasions there was the odd fall on the way home because of the dark. That was my first experience on Inis Oir and I spent over 30 years working out there.

Other people that looked after us so well were Mr and Mrs Poill (RIP), Maggie Willie and Padraic Cait (RIP) who I stayed with during my time working on the island.

I worked on Inis Mor in 1975. There were a crew of 6-7 lads sent out on a Wednesday and I was going the following Saturday. I was meeting a lad in Taaffe's Bar in Galway who was taking me out on the trawler from the docks. When I went to meet him in the pub he said: "What are you having?" That was at 7am.

I spent about four months working on Inis Mor with Brid and Colie Connolly looking after me for years. It was a home from home and they turned out to be great friends. Brid did all the cleaning and washing and fed me well. In later years I stayed with Penny Mahon in Tigh Fitz who also looked after me very well. I started work on the Sunday after mass and worked for about four months, getting home one weekend every month. During this time we employed a number of the islanders who were some characters.

We would have a pint at night with the locals. I recall being in the pub and Paddy Quinn coming in after fishing and throwing a salmon on the floor, one that had been nipped by otters and couldn't be sold. We cooked it for our dinner the following day.

One Saturday night we walked into the pub and there sitting in the middle of it were two Honda 50s. The lads didn't want them to go missing!

I had little or no Irish going to the islands and some of our work involved erecting pole struts. These were poles mounted on rock, which the islanders called cossai fada.

I worked for a short period in Inis Mean, staying in various places on the island. There was one pub – 'Pádraic's'. The islanders had very little English so it was a good way of having to pick up the Irish language.

The roads on the island were very narrow so if you met an oncoming vehicle, someone had to reverse. One day we were coming along the road and we met an ass and cart. Peadar Mor got off the cart, lifted the cart into the ditch and gave the ass a kick in the backside and he jumped into the ditch so the ESB van could pass.

I also did a stint on Omey Island. There were four houses there at that time and it became cut off from the mainland at high tide. You had to watch for the tide coming in or else you would be stranded there for the night as was often the case.

Inishbofin was another island I spent time working on. When we arrived on the island we started to unload Paddy Halloran's boat with the help of the islanders. They had lined up looking for work. One of the lads with me said: 'We should take on the old man with the cap'. When I showed reluctance and asked why, he explained: "It's because he looks like he could keep manners on the young lads". We took him on and he did just that.

However there was one young lad and we were hiring him whether we liked it or not. He was a young child from the island and every morning when we'd come out he would be sitting in the van with the blue hard hat on waiting to start work. He spent many a day with us, happily watching us work.

There were not many cars on the island and there were three elderly local men who would walk down for their pint at night. I'd say to one of the lads: "You wouldn't go over and pick up the three lads." One of them was a real character and when he was asked how did he get to the pub, he'd proudly respond: "Sure didn't I get a lift in the BBC van."

I made many friends on Innisboffin and still visit the island each year with my wife and children.

My years working on the islands were very special to me and I developed such a bond with the islands and islanders. While some of those islanders are now deceased, it is lovely to see their children and families still living there and keeping the traditions alive.

I smile whenever I see na cossai fada still holding erect ESB poles against the might of Atlantic gales.

Mick Grealish is a native of Galway with a wealth of memories from a lifetime of working on the islands for the ESB. He is a former rugby coach who was president of Connacht rugby in 2008-9.

"My mother filled it with pink paraffin oil and I watched the wick curl down into the glass orb and just lie there soaking up the oil. Everything about it was blue and delicate."

Rita Kelly – 'Then It Happened'

41

'Then It Happened...'
Rita Kelly

IT was velvet black; I couldn't even see my mother as we walked to Lucy Bourke's house, so I linked her. We could see a car lights miles away in the sky, it was so far away, we might never see it, it might never pass us.

Lucy had offered my mother the loan of an oil lamp, which we could have until the electricity arrived. We were going to collect it. It was a beautiful object. My mother filled it with pink paraffin oil and I watched the wick curl down into the glass orb and just lie there soaking up the oil. Everything about it was blue and delicate. There was blue work on the stand that was sturdy, my mother adjusted the two turning handles to increase the light or decrease it. Then she placed the glass tube ever so gently over that flame and into a set of brass teeth which held it firmly in place.

We had a Tilley lamp too, used mostly to keep the foxes away from the newborn lambs. It was a really strong light; there was a mantel, there was a brass pump and there was a clip thing with two blocks of absorbent material which was soaked in purple methylated spirits before setting it under the mantel and lighting it. The Tilley hissed all the time; unlike Lucy's lamp, which made light and made shadows in the quiet of the kitchen.

After months and months, it happened. They were coming, the men with the electricity. My father and mother were delighted, something from the modern life and no more messing with paraffin and mantels. My father visited old relations at night, grey-haired men and women who sat around an open fire listening to the crickets – a sign of rain, most things were a sign of rain – sometimes in candlelight, sometimes in lamp light, a little tin thing which needed constant filling; or they just sat in the firelight.

Sometimes my father took me on those visits.

"Well, Peter, I'm not sure at all about this electric yoke. I heard there was a house near Eyrecourt and the electric cooker was dancing around the floor when they came home."

"Might have been lightening."

"Jay, you couldn't have a yoke like that in the house, jumping and spitting sparks and pulling itself out of the wall."

So it went on, the fears and the misgivings; the cost, the inconvenience. But I couldn't hide my excitement. It was autumn, I rushed home from school in the quiet, gentle air of September wondering had they come yet?

Then they came, lots of them, men and machines. They dug deep holes and threw up beautiful black clay. They dug a hole near the yard wall, close to the house and the sheds. There were long black poles, treated to preserve them. They were raised in place.

That was a big operation, long before the wires came, the poles had to be steadied and firmed in the ground. There was a great deal of heaving and discussing and pulling things this way and that way. Further up the field they put a big wire at an angle to the pole to steady it. My father wasn't too mad about that, as it was in the way when cutting hay. It turned out that their engineer was a cousin of my father's from Clara, in Co Offaly. He was Owen Clyne, young and very nice. So there was a lot of talk, stories and laughter. Vast amounts of tea were drunk and all these men filled our kitchen with shadows and talk. They couldn't get enough of my mother's brown and white bread.

"Soon you'll have the electric oven."

"No time for it. I will still bake in my Stanley range, easier to regulate," my mother said.

Owen asked my father if they could store the equipment in our barn.

"Absolutely," said my father.

They were all delighted, lots more talk. Big men brought all kinds of equipment into the barn. The huge spools with cable they brought off with them as it had its own trailer. The letters ESB were burned into everything, all the wooden ladders and other wooden items. My father told me that they used wooden ladders because it didn't conduct electricity like metal did, so if there were a problem the person wouldn't get electrocuted. That certainly frightened me. Electrocution. You could get that from lightening as well.

You would get all black and burned if the lightening hit you. You had to lie down if you got caught in it. I got soaked lying in the pouring rain, in our field away from the house. The thunder was so loud. My father said electricity and lightening were the same things, all energy.

I was totally fascinated by the big metal shoes with teethed hooks the men used to climb up the poles. It was like magic. You didn't need a ladder at all. You just walked up the pole and walked down again.

So after much planning in my head and a thorough sense that I could succeed and the result would be marvellous, I took the climbing shoes, one at a time, because of their weight, and dragged them to the nearest pole. I knew I had a clear run; my mother and my father were either gone somewhere or fully occupied.

Very carefully I put a foot into the big metal frame. It was of course miles too big for me. It felt like a huge trap that hung under the thatch in what was known as 'the coach house.' I then bent down to fit my left foot in. God, they were heavy and awkward when I tried to move. I almost fell forward with the weight of them and then I almost fell backwards when I tried to right myself. I was determined now.

I grabbed the pole and tried to lift up my right foot. It was such an effort and then the climbing shoe just slid down the pole. Again and again that happened, even when I tried my left foot, the same thing. I was almost in tears now with the effort and the frustration. I could see the teeth on the curved hook of the climbing shoe, but they just slid down the pole. I thought that there had to be a knack. Something missing, something I am not doing...then just by accident the hook gripped. What had happened? Yes, something had. I discovered that I had flicked my foot in a certain way and the teeth dug into the timber.

I could almost hear it, I could certainly feel it. It was great, it took away all the awkward weight and I was standing solidly on one foot and on one climbing shoe. I got the other one up. And then took the next step. They were short steps, but I was progressing, I was succeeding. I was looking down on the shiny galvanized roof of the cow shed. I could only look in certain directions. There was too much to concentrate on, the shoes, the weight, the next step, holding on with my arms. The ground and the grass under me were getting further away. I didn't know the word 'exhilarating' then, but that's what it was, definitely.

I was doing something magical, I was going above the yard, the sheds and the fields. I could see a tuft of grass growing in the eves. I was alone. I might die, but I didn't think so. I might get caught, then I certainly would be killed, but I would have that feeling of exhilaration forever. I threw back my head and looked up to the top of the pole. How far could I go, I wondered? There were two shiny galvanized footrests up there. If I got that far I would have to get out of the climbing shoes to stand on them. A lot of flustering, it could be awkward, could be dangerous. Just when my head was near the footrests and I could see around me over the hedges, across the fields, over the walls, but not behind me, too difficult, I became a little tired and said to myself, time to get down now. I was way above our garden wall; I could see the pattern of the uneven stones on the top.

No matter how hard I tried to flick my foot to get the climbing shoe off the pole, it just wouldn't move. I tried for ages; at first one foot, then the other, then back to the first. It wouldn't budge.

The teeth were well embedded in the pole. I was tired now and afraid. If they come back and find me... if they come back and don't find me... all over I was tired. And I knew that when you're in trouble and not succeeding you get even more tired.

I decided there was only one solution. It had to work, though I never did it before. If I stayed calm but did it quickly it would work. No going back. I couldn't change my mind once I had started.

So I undid the straps across my shoes. When both were undone, I stepped off, got my legs around the pole, took a deep breath and shimmied down to earth.

Oh the relief. Oh the terror looking up at the climbing shoes. Now the world would know. I was on the ground but I would be killed.

Strangely no one ever mentioned the pole or the climbing shoes.

Never. And the electric light lit up everywhere within. Like magic, it was a warm light, as the winter set in.

Rita Kelly is an award-winning poet from East Galway who now lives in Tramore, Co Waterford.

42

Saboteurs Who Kept Us In The Dark

Eamon Ginnane

R URAL electrification came to the townlands of Moyarta and Rahona and the village of Carrigaholt in County Clare in 1951. I was a teenager at the time and remember quite distinctly when the man was sent out from the ESB to determine how many lights each household wanted.

Most asked for only one light with the odd prosperous home opting for multiple lights. I remember seeing my neighbour Paddy Hedderman out in the field discussing at length with the ESB man how many he should get before finally agreeing on one.

The good news in a countryside bereft of much employment was that holes needed to be dug for the electricity poles. Work was available to the unemployed and small farmers once they were willing to swing a pick axe and dig holes with shovels.

My older brother Thomas was one such lucky person to find employment in this way. They paid a set amount per pole and plenty got opportunities to make money because it was a very labour-intensive process.

His supervisors were helpful and provided wellingtons for the mucky, swampy ground. Working hours lasted from 8am-4pm.

It changed my brother's life. Thomas continued working with the ESB until he had earned sufficient money for his passage to London and eventually to New York.

You could say he went from digging holes at home to working for Chase Manhattan Bank in New York, where he remained until his retirement. It was indeed a long, long way from Clare to there.

The ESB was astute as they offered those who were hard workers further employment in other parishes after their own area was finished.

The official switch on for the village was arranged for St. Mary's Parish Hall in Carrigaholl. Everybody was in great humour and waiting anxiously for the big moment. It was organised so that the oldest person available would symbolically quench a candle and the youngest child would turn on the light switch.

The Parish Priest of Carrigaholt, Fr. John Cleary, was the oldest man in the hall that night, so it fell on him to quench the candle. Then the youngest child hit the switch and...nothing happened. A big 'aw' emanated from the crowd followed by fits of nervous laughter.

Fr. Cleary called out for a volunteer to check with the Garda Station next door to see if they had any power. When the volunteer returned he replied: "No power there either. Let's go back to the old reliable candle."

It took 90 minutes before the light finally came on. Fr. Cleary apologised for the delay but immediately assured residents that despite the fault on the first night, electricity would create a bright future for them.

It took two days for the news to break as to what caused the power failure. Some people threw a separate wire cable across the main ESB wires leading to the village from the Kilkee direction. The wire was earthed to a piece of steel driven into the ground in a field parallel to the Moyarta graveyard.

After this came to light, the ESB issued a statement warning the perpetrators that they could have been electrocuted. The culprits were never arrested despite the best efforts of the Gardai. In fact the saboteurs, whoever they were, took their secret with them to the next world.

Eamon Ginnane is a native of Carrigaholt, County Clare and an avid supporter of Banner teams. Retired after over 40 years service in the Post Office in Athlone and Longford, he is married with two daughters.

43

Spreading The Hurling Message To The West

Seán Mac Fearghail

T IM SLEVIN was born on the 14 July 1929 in Kilregane in the parish of Lorrha in Tipperary into a family of 16 children. He learned and honed his hurling skills on the GAA pitches of the parish at 'Blakefield' and 'The Pike'. Timmy hurled for Lorrha at under 14, 16 and minor level in the 1940s.

He was greatly inspired by the great clubman and Tipperary star goalkeeper Tony Reddan, who won three All Ireland medals with Tipp and was later selected on the 'Team of the Century' in 1984 and on the 'Team of the Millennium' in 2000.

In 1950, Rural Electrification Scheme came to the parish of Lorrha. Tim joined an installation crew. When the local scheme was completed he moved to the Cork District and worked in parishes around Carrigaline.

From there he moved to the Sligo district – a big geographical sweep taking in counties Mayo, Sligo, North Roscommon, Leitrim and Donegal.

After that, his next stop on the scheme was Mountcharles in Co. Donegal. The ESB crews erected over 2000 poles between Mountcharles and Teelin Bay in 1951 and 1952 during two of the toughest winters ever experienced. By 1952 over 450 houses had been wired up to the National Grid.

The following year Tim was on the move again, this time to Charlestown. One of his colleagues suggested Mrs Fitzgerald's Guest House there for his digs but when they called she was away and her daughter Tina was in charge. After much persuading and cajoling by his friend and the charm of the good-looking young stranger, Tina agreed to take in the 'ESB lodger'. There must have been a great ESB spark that day as the young Tipp man married Mrs Fitzgerald's daughter, Tina, in Knock in 1959.

Tim brought another great love with him when he moved from Tipperary – hurling. He won a Mayo county hurling medal playing for Belmullet in 1956. Barry Ormond from Waterford, who was an esteemed ESB colleague of Tim's, also played a starring role in winning that first championship for Belmullet.

With so many parishes in the country to be hooked up to the new electricity scheme, the ESB men and their wives were always on the move.

Tim and Tina's next location was Ballinamore in Co. Leitrim in September 1959 and Barry also moved there. Almost immediately the pair started to coach the locals on the basic skills of hurling. There wasn't a lot of interest initially. Ballinamore was the leading football club in Leitrim and had no tradition of hurling.

The two lads continued to manage the erection of poles, hanging copper wires and the installation of transformers during the day. In the evenings they coached and trained the locals.

Before long well-known footballers like Paddy Dolan, Sean Kavanagh, Dermot Gannon and Michael McCarthy had started to swing a camán. They were also joined in practice games by Gerry Mahon, (future Hurling Board Chairman), Pat Cull, Paddy Friel, and Galway native Seán Flaherty. Hurling took hold in the area.

Tim and Barry spent hours in Pairc Seán Ó Heslin coaching, mentoring and encouraging young lads from the area to take up the game.

Tim spent from September 1959 until September 1963 rolling out electricity to the parishes surrounding Ballinamore. The names of some of these parishes like Corraleehan, Aughawillan, Fenagh, Carrigallen, and Mohill would become household names a few years later through the writings of the author John McGahern.

However, it was not all about poles, copper wires and hurling, there was also time for romance. This was the era of the great dancing boom in the early 1960s when the original 'Ballroom of Romance' in Glenfarne was in its heyday. Dance halls like the 'Wonderland' in Bawnboy, 'The Star' in Ballyconnell, 'The Mayflower' in Drumshambo, and the first ballroom that Albert Reynolds built, 'The Cloudland' in Rooskey were rocking every Sunday night to bands like Brendan Bowyer and Larry Cunningham and the Mighty Avons.

The single lads from the ESB were a great hit with the young girls and were not shy in showing their dancing skills. There were romances and even marriages.

Barry, the dashing young wing-half from Waterford, did not escape. He met and married the lovely Ann Brady from Ballinamore in the early sixties. Barry was a great exponent of the 'Huckle Buck' and when he popped the question, how could she refuse? Barry and Ann are now retired and living in South Dublin.

In September of 1963 Tim, Tina and their young family moved to Mohill on the next phase of rural electrification in adjoining parishes. He also moved on to the next phase of his hurling career.

In the spring of 1964 the hurling championship in the county was close to collapsing and would have done so only for the intervention of a group of hurling enthusiasts from Ballinamore, Cloone, Fenagh, and Mohill – the St Finbarr's Hurling club was born.

Later that year Tim pulled on the No 3 jersey for St Finbarr's and won his first Leitrim Senior Hurling championship medal.

They won their second title the following year, with Tim as captain and Barry wearing the No 10 jersey and in '66 completed the three-in-a-row.

St Finbarr's won their fourth title in '68 and in 1969 Leitrim won the Connacht Junior Hurling championship for the first time ever in a team backboned by players from St Finbarr's.

They also won another Leitrim championship that year – a fifth medal for Tim.

By 1979 St Finbarr's and Timmy had won their eighth Leitrim senior medal. That year it was all of 36 years since he first pulled on a hurling jersey to play for his native Lorrha at U-14 level.

Tim gave the ESB 45 years of wonderful service and by working on the rural electrification roll out, helped to transplant hurling into an area of Leitrim that until his arrival, had little regard for hurling.

You could say the Mohill resident had put the small ball on the map in this area between the poles he also helped to erect as part of the scheme.

Seán Mac Fearghail is a passionate Leitrim man and a former Gaelic footballer. He had the unique distinction of never missing a day's work during almost 44 years as an Aer Lingus employee. He is an avid follower of national and international sports.

44

The Bere Facts Of The Case

John Finbarr O'Sullivan

I WAS born, grew up on Bere Island and in 1949 I got a motor apprenticeship in Peter Murphy Senior's garage in Castletownbere. That was a few years before the Rural Electrification Scheme came to the Beara Peninsula.

Bill Sheehan (RIP) was one of the mechanics working in the garage who was also a brilliant electrician. Mr. Murphy sent Bill out wiring houses and sent me along as his helper. We wired houses in Castletownbere, Eyeries, Urhan and Allihies and the people treated us royally.

I learned a lot from Bill. I usually went up into the attic laying out the cables. We had to bore holes in the joists with a carpenter's brace and bit. There were no battery operated drills in those days. That was hard work especially in some houses where the joists were 3" x 4" or 4" x 4" oak or pitch pine which was usually wreckage from a ship. In one of the houses when we tried to run a cable down on the internal partition, we discovered that it was packed with turf.

In the mid-1950s I was back in Bere Island when some people petitioned the ESB to bring electricity to the Island. The company couldn't spare a gang so they made up a special small unit to do Bere Island.

Paddy Moynihan was the supervisor, Jim Lavers was one of the electricians and they had a few local workers to help with the hard work. The underwater cable was laid by the late Brendan Murphy of Rerrin from his barge. To avail of the scheme people needed to have their houses wired. As I had all the necessary skills required from my time with Bill Sheehan, I put everything I had learned to good use.

I loaded up my bicycle, two bags of cables and fittings hanging from the handlebars, a box with tools on the carrier and a few lengths of wooden conduit tied to the crossbar. I wasn't the only one doing this work but personally I wired 65 houses and gave back change out of a £10 note in 63 of them. That price included labour and all materials except the bulbs.

I got my dinner in every house. As a thank you, I wired and fitted a red sacred heart bulb free of charge. They all said they would say a prayer for me.

Some of the houses in Rerrin village had 110 volt electricity from the British Army until 1938 and then from the Irish Army. When I was rewiring one of those houses, I found bare copper wires... the mice had eaten the rubber insulation.

In another house, when I'd finished the wiring, I asked the elderly man of the house to switch on the light in the kitchen. He switched it on and off a few times and said: "Glory be to God! When I was young the only light we had was seal blubber melted in a scallop shell and a dried rush for a wick".

Here was a man born in the early 1880s who survived long enough to witness the extraordinary times that the Rural Electrification brought to the islanders of Bere.

John Finbarr O'Sullivan is a writer, folklorist and native of Bere Island, Co Cork.

45

Lighting The First Christmas Tree In Ballivor

Maureen McGearty

MY father was alive when the first canvass for the electricity came to Ballivor in 1951 but by the time the work began and lights were installed two years later he was dead.

My mother had eight of us to rear. We had two cows, two calves and nine or 10 acres of land. My father died without making a will – it took 16 years before we got his affairs in order – but my mother, bless her forward thinking, decided that we'd get the electricity in like most other houses in the place.

However we didn't use the services of the local electrician because we couldn't afford to. Instead my brother, who was only 18 at the time, wired the house from top to bottom with a little help from other members of the family.

It is testament to his standards of understanding what was required that not only was the work passed by the ESB people at the time but quite recently when I got the same house rewired over 60 years later, the electrician said he had seldom come across such perfect installation.

We lived next door in Ballivor to the Catholic Church and it was decided that after getting the electricity installed in 1953 that we would use the power from our house to light up a Christmas tree on the street that holiday season. The reason we made that decision was because the street lights weren't operational in the town until the following year and we took the responsibility on ourselves to light the way.

I'm sure by today's lighting and displays, it was a very humble offering but we thought it was great at the time.

Myself and my sister sewed cotton wool tufts along black thread to create the impression of snow and my brother Patsy sourced fairy lights to put around the top of the tree.

We plugged it into the socket and it was the eighth wonder of the world the way people stopped and looked at this shining creation on Main Street, Ballivor as they made their way to and from midnight mass and all the other masses that year.

Although there were street lights in by the following year, our family continued with the tradition of lighting the Christmas Tree from our house for a quarter of a century. We stopped only when we got the fright of our lives after a crack in the cable went unseen. It meant that the church railings were all 'live' one year and it was only the grace of God that no one was electrocuted.

Needless to say, we passed on the responsibility after that... but it was a pleasure for our family of eight – all still alive – to have added to the light in Ballivor for 25 years each Christmas.

Maureen McGearty is a native of Ballivor, Co Meath. A contemporary of writer John Quinn, she taught some of the Saw Doctors while working in Tuam, Co Galway.

46

The Sunken World Of The River Lee

Eileen Ludlow

I AM sure it was much more difficult for those who lived along the river Lee to imagine what benefits would emerge in their daily lives from this new fangled thing called "the electric." Many of these people were to see some of their land go under water. This land was to be flooded to power the dams at Inniscarra and Carrigadrohid.

This was no ordinary flooding caused by an act of God but was to be a permanent one. Not just land either; in some cases houses and business premises went under as well.

The tranquil Lee was to change forever more. We lost the shallow crossing points along the river where my father and his neighbours walked from their home in Annahala through the Gearagh. This was a place of outstanding natural and environmental value, full of ancient oaks and pines. Alas, this too became part of the lake behind the Carrigadrohid dam.

People who had lived there for generations were compensated for their loss which came at a cost to us all. They had a natural attachment to the land and were devastated by the prospect of its submergence.

One man who lived in the Gearagh refused to leave his cottage. Fortunately it was high enough not to be flooded but it was an island in the new landscape and his only means of crossing to the mainland was by a small rowing boat. His smallholding went under and all he had left was a barn yard.

The Lee Scheme, as it was called, was a great advance, powering the rural Lee valley and surrounding countryside.

There were rumours of pending disaster. One such tale that

reached our ears as children was the prediction that Cork city would be washed away when the dam at Inniscarra burst its banks.

Every time my mother went shopping into the city my younger sister would wait anxiously for her return in case she got washed away.

Construction of the dams at Carrigadrohid and Inniscarra gave employment to many former farm workers. Here the money was better even if the work was harder. The going rate for a farm labourer in those days was £4 a week. I am sure of this because as an eight year old I had the job of putting the money under the sugar bowl for Con who worked on the farm and came in for his tea of boiled egg and homemade bread and jam before he went home on Saturday night.

Con was a very knowledgeable man and I was often intrigued to tune into his conversations with my grandmother. He did not like the idea of the land being flooded, especially his brother's farm where he was born and raised. He could see no need for such drastic change to put a light switch on a wall.

It was a way of life around this tiny stream which rose in the mountain behind Gougane Barra before meandering through the countryside to the Gearagh. It was shallow enough in places for people to cross on foot or on horseback on route to school, to shop, to go to Mass and to the pub. From here it travelled through very fertile farmland under stone bridges on to Carrigadrohid and from there to Rooves Bridge. It flowed then on through more good land to Inniscarra and the Lee fields to meet the sea at Cork harbour. The story goes, that it was the route that St Finbarr took on his way from his monastery in Gougane Barra to found Cork City in the marsh at the mouth of the river.

There is, of course, no way back to find what is under the waters of today's River Lee except in older people's memories. Back to when I was a child of eight, a time when far away places first enjoyed this new electricity. Life was slow. The year 1954 was The Marian Year and many children including boys were given Mary as a second name. Grottos to Our Lady were constructed in many parishes along the Lee Valley.

The building of the dams were progressing and houses were being prepared and wired for connection.

The emigrants were not happy about their homestead being flooded. They had got on with their lives abroad and enjoyed all the benefits of electricity but they did not want any changes around their native heaths.

The emphasis was on the landscape becoming a lake, with new roads and new bridges; all that was familiar was gone.

My aunt was the proud owner of a Ford Prefect car and took me with her on her outings of discovery. One such journey was to see the dam being built at Inniscarra. I didn't find it very exciting and didn't understand its significance at that stage.

A trip that had a much greater impact on me was to see the new Rooves Bridge – it appeared to be almost floating up there in the sky. It made no sense to me that the bridge we were standing on and the pub beside it was going to vanish forever.

The past, the present and the future were there that day as I stood on that old stone bridge. It was as if two worlds were set apart by two bridges, one to vanish and one to dominate.

Yet I feel this world I grew up in is still there under the dark waters. In it, there are men riding their bikes home from the pub and the local guard is trying to catch out the after-hour drinker who claims to be a bona fide traveller who lives over three miles away.

The local postman who knows everyone and carries news as well as post is on his bike too. The drover is there, driving stock to Coachford Fair in the early hours.

In the evenings there are crowds in this underworld making their way to the pitch in Coachford to shout for the parish team.

Near Macroom there is the remains of a stone bridge that appears and disappears as the flood water rises and falls.

It's a sign of the life that once was and for some, a sign of a life that still is.

Eileen Ludlow is a native of Farran, Co Cork but has lived in Meath for over 40 years where she is a holistic therapist. She is married to Peter and they have three grown up children and five grandchildren. She enjoys jotting down stories from her childhood.

"When they referred to electricity, it meant as much to me as a desert would to Noah and his Arc. Then as the years turned into the 1950s the word on everyone's lips was 'light.'"

**Alec Byrne –
'A Washing Machine Conundrum'**

47

A Washing Machine Conundrum

Alec Byrne

I WAS a child of the 1940s who grew up in the Glen of the Downs in Wicklow. At home at night our world was lit by matches, lamps and candles. When I went to school, the townies only talked of sockets and switches – we might as well have been speaking two different languages.

When they referred to electricity, it meant as much to me as a desert would to Noah and his Arc. Then as the years turned into the 1950s the word on everyone's lips was 'light.'

"Are you getting the light?"

A man in our area not only worked in the ESB – he was "high up" and the word was he had the power to turn our darkness into light.

All that was needed was a canvass of the district to get enough people willing to have the electric into their homes.

I was only a chap then seeing this unfold was reminiscent of looking for votes at a general election. You had those voting for, those dead against the 'don't knows' who waited until their minds were made up for them. The fifties were indeed lean times and was the last decade without regular bills – no phones, no cars, no insurance, no standing orders.

The ESB bill was probably the first regular draw on a house's finances and that turned some heads against the scheme too.

With so many thatched houses then, others were genuinely afraid that if they got the electricity in, it would burn down their home around them.

The canvassers were for the light and all over the country they met those who agreed to get the light so that they could find candles and matches if it was dark. They also put forward the benefits of water inside the house though many were told by householders that the biggest job they had was spending half the winter keeping the cursed water out.

My memory of that time is a true story. When the canvassers came to this man's door, they extolled the virtues of light and the accoutrements that would make life easier for all who bought them.

Trying to get the right side of the woman as well, they mentioned the advantages of having a washing machine in the house.

"I'll stop ya there," said the man with his hand up. "I was in a place across the way the other night and one of those washing yokes ye speak of was in the kitchen. And as sure as I'm standing here, I've never seen two dirtier chaps in all my life in that home – so don't tell me the washing machine works, because it doesn't."

Alec Byrne, (72) was born in the Glen of the Downs, Co Wicklow and has lived there all his life on the family farm. He is married with two grown up children.

48

'God Is Understanding Of Progress'

Noel King

KITTY watched the flicker in the dark from the new Sacred Heart light at the end of the stairs; her lips moving in quiet prayer and the odd crackle from her fire the only sounds. With his steps at last outside she grasped her beads more firmly, sat up to face him.

Her son-in-law switched on the light and blinked back momentarily at her. "Still up, Mrs?" he mumbled. She didn't respond or hear his retorts on why she'd sit in the dark, as he tore off his boots and pulled himself, panting – and briefly blocking her view – up the stairs. She blessed herself, grabbed a tea-towel and with a nervous hand pushed down the smooth, black switch by the back door.

She jumped at the click, then was at peace again in the dark. On the stairs she became careful without the light from her oil lamp only today made redundant. Careful too of new, unfamiliar chips, children's toys that could be lying there. From the top, she saw the Sacred Heart from a new position and stared at the blank marks where the photographs of her mother and father had not yet been replaced.

Kitty passed to her room, splashed some barely warm water into her mother's pink flower bowl, felt egg stains on the white linen cloth as she dried, and undressed. Making the sign of the cross on her grandchildren's foreheads, she slipped in beside the eldest. She had always slipped in beside someone in this very bed; her older sister, her younger sister; her husband, Joe; and now her grandchildren.

It was winter so Kitty prayed in bed, before turning on her side and pressing her eyes shut. They were soon open again remembering her mother's reaction when they both saw their first motor car. If there was a moon Kitty would have seen her sunflower wallpaper hanging in torn strips.

She wondered what class of paper they'd put up now? Kitty had failed to busy herself today as men hacked her house. No stranger had ever been in her room before, had ever moved her bed and dresser or scratched them roughly back into position. A visit to a cousin in Dublin 20 years ago came to her; the bright lights she saw there, the floodlit music hall with her namesake, Kate Captaw, performing all those songs Kitty had heard on Mr. Maddox's radio when she went to clean for him.

On arriving home, her beloved Joe – lying where her granddaughter lay now – had put his arms around her, told her he smelt the city off her, and didn't like it. But he'd been glad she'd gone.

She had stayed silent when her son-in-law announced they were getting 'the gadget.' Fr O'Connor had said at Mass that everyone should get it, that 'twas time for it. A distant cousin's visit in the spring of 1926 turned to tears when she took 'small Kitty', her first born, off to America with her.

That started what Fr. O'Connor told her mothers all over the country had to contend with, as the two middle daughters followed the next years. Kitty's baby carrying on the line, as Joe called it, was something she still prayed thanks for each day. She 'loves' and appreciates her son-in-law, delighting in her youngest child's happiness.

Sleep hadn't come when, with her grandchildren moving about the room, Kitty rose to her duties, blinking in the unnatural light in the room.

"Holy God, who put that on? Why did the Lord give us daylight?"

"But, you can see better now Nana." Her grandmother scoffed taking the hairbrush to the girls' heads, her favourite routine.

"You look tired Mod, didn't you sleep?" her daughter asked.

"Ah sure, how would anyone sleep with the lives around us changin' like 'tis... are we outa oatenmeal?" She upturned the white tin.

With the girls gone to school, Kitty gave her grandson his breakfast and as her daughter suckled the younger baby she slowly went round the house examining each black circle with the little switch in the middle. Her eyes tried to follow the wire, but jumped back to source. Again she started, hand holding the table. Her vision blurred into several lines. She made tea, shut eyes by the fire, and started again. This time with close, slow precision she followed each wire across the ceiling to its exit.

Her grandson was a small help feeding the chickens. A neighbour man came into the yard, patted the child's head and followed Kitty to the kitchen. She smoked a cigarette with him as they drank her daughter's tea. "How's the blasted gadget going for ye?" was all he wanted to know. He went on to swear he'd gotten a shock from the thing the night before.

"Have ta be careful, Mike," she said, "don't catch it with wet hands, whatever ye do." He worried too if the bill would go up in no time at all.

As dusk fell Kitty screamed seeing the eldest child handle it. The child smirked, Kitty wants to hear: "Hush Nana, it's all right" or "Hush Nana, it's safe" or even "Hush Nana, I am allowed" but the child hadn't noticed any reaction. Kitty's hands covered her face in her chair. The child took a book, sat on the bottom stair, a new position for reading.

Her son-in-law shaved in silence, then emptied coins from the jam jar behind the clock and took off amid a 'time for bed' argument between his wife and children. Later her daughter spoke to Kitty excitedly about the neighbours she'd seen during her day, how Annie Finn only switched it on to see her way lighting the gas, how Jack Dardis counted 96 feet of wiring going into his house.

"Mary Jameson said that her mother went to bed as soon as they'd put it on. T'wasn't natural, she said." Kitty didn't reply, stared from her fire to the roots on her daughters bent head and the purple shades of colour developing in her knitting.

Later she sat at the table with a library book, Mansfield Park, her fifth or sixth time. Jane Austen, what would she have thought of all this light? Kitty chuckled. "Mod, why don't you bring your book closer to the fire, 'tis bright enough here now for readin'."

He was later again coming home. Again she blinked in the light. Did Toby Maguire have longer opening hours now with the gadget? she wanted to ask. Or is it that the black stuff is sweeter in the light?

"Must be frozen, woman," he said, "fire's gone out." Towelling his damp hair he turned for the kettle. Propping his head on one hand, he sucked tea and gulped brown bread. She couldn't look at the ruddy glow on his cheeks.

She saw him 10 years before, that very table, her daughter in love.

Their happiness mattered to Joe: "But Kitty, she's 23," Joe'd said. "Can't let her folley d'others to America. What would one of us do in our ould age?"

"Suppose you'll be wantin' it switched off again?" Her son in law's voice startled her.

"Aaah, I'll be goin' up in a minute."

"Could bring back th'auld lamp if 'twould plase ya?"

Sunday evening she took the eldest child, a girl, the long way round to the top of the hill, refusing to go under those new wires on ugly poles. Together they watched lights go on in six neighbouring households.

"Why's ours not on yet, Nana?"

"Don't know love, maybe.... Aah there, there 'tis."

The child smiled, relieved.

She expected him earlier on Sunday night. It was past midnight. She had dozed off. Had she sleeping trouble again he wanted to know. She shrugged: "No, but just 'tisn't the same as 'twas. The man above never meant us to have this."

"Ah, but God is understandin' of progress... that's what Fr O'Connor calls it, progress."

The day of the Christmas holidays Kitty stood as usual at the outside light 'til she heard their voices, then placed thick cut slices of white bread over the fire. Her daughter pulled the baby from her breast and covered herself. The baby began to cry. His sisters rushed to his attention. A cold hand wiped over his dribble.

"Warm ye're selves. And wash ye're hands before handling the baby," their mother shouted. Her husband was home; fixing a hole under a press from where the girls said that mouse had come on Saturday night.

It was then the bang came. The sudden darkness. The girls got frightened. Their father cursed the loss of the wireless. It wouldn't be for long their mother assured them, the man would come and fix it in the morning.

Kitty turned the toast, browned it lightly and began to scrape on butter.

Noel King was born and lives in Tralee, Co Kerry. In this his 50th year, he has reached his 1000th publication of a poem, haiku or short story in magazines and journals in thirty-eight countries. A short story collection, The Key Signature & Other Stories will be published by Liberties Press in 2017.

"The stark reality was staring him in the face, which was to do what many others like him had to do. This was to leave his wife and family behind and take the boat to England or Scotland in order to provide a living for his family."

John McArt – 'When A Few Weeks' Work Turned Into 40 Years'

49

When A Few Weeks' Work Turned Into 40 Years

John McArt

A T the age of 34, my father Pat McArt sold up a small subsistence farm that he owned in a rural part of Donegal and with the proceeds he purchased a house a few miles away in the town of Raphoe.

The year was 1950. He moved with his wife and two young children but had no job. He searched relentlessly for work but with no success.

The stark reality was staring him in the face, which was to do what many others like him had to do. This was to leave his wife and family behind and take the boat to England or Scotland in order to provide a living for his family.

Early the following year as he was making final plans to make the journey abroad to seek work, he had a chance meeting with a neighbour to whom he explained his predicament.

Fortunately a few days later this same neighbour came to see my father and informed him that there was a man sitting in a lorry up in the Diamond in Raphoe. He was seeking workers for something to do with electricity.

My father immediately made his way up to the Diamond and got talking to the man in the lorry. He explained to this man how he was new to the town and was desperately seeking work.

The man sympathised with him but informed him that at that stage he had recruited all the men he needed. As my father walked away bitterly disappointed, the man called him back and said: "Seeing as you are a stranger here like myself, I will give you a start. Turn up for work here at 8am next Monday morning and you will get a few weeks."

Those few words started a 40-year association with the ESB for my father.

He very much enjoyed his first week working on 'rural,' meeting new work colleagues and getting a sense of what this new concept of rural electrification was all about. He could equally recall his first weeks wages; £3-17-1 (three pounds, seventeen shillings and one penny). This was very good wages for that time and that type of work. He was even more ecstatic when within a short period of time his wages were increased to four pounds and nine shillings.

This again was an exceptional wage when compared to what county council workers got for similar work. It was no wonder I reminded him that the family quickly grew from the two children he had when he started with the ESB to seven within a relatively short period of time!

His very first assignment in January 1951 was to work with the gang of men who were employed in bringing the 38 line, as it was known, through the Barnesmore Gap.

This was the line that was instrumental in lighting up many homes in Donegal for the very first time with electricity. He went on to work in many other parts of the county as they blazed a trail of lighting up a whole county for the first time.

He recalled that they were not always welcomed with open arms as some people were opposed to the introduction of new-fangled things into their homes, which many believed to be both dangerous and costly. A common refrain was – "aren't we grand the way we are?"

He remembered many stories from sales staff who had the task of introducing electricity into rural Donegal. One salesman who was trying to get an elderly lady to purchase an electric kettle went through the process of demonstrating the speed the kettle could boil the water and went on to make the lady of the house a nice pot of tea. She thanked him politely but there was no way he could persuade the lady to drink the tea. She was adamant that she would get electrocuted from water boiled by electricity.

He also recalled being told by another salesman about persuading a householder to introduce electric light into their home. On a return he asked the lady of the house did she use the electric light much? Her reply was; "Oh God we do, we put it on for a few minutes every evening when we are lighting the Tilley Lamp." This was the reality of the time, people had genuine fears and concerns.

There was also little money available. Electricity incurred a standing charge, a usage charge; there were fears that a spark from an electric cable could burn down their thatched cottage or they themselves could get electrocuted from using electric appliances. These fears had to be addressed and overcome by good and innovative sales people at that time.

Much of the work of excavating deep holes, erecting poles and installing lines, that the gang of men my father was involved with was done in atrocious weather conditions, with little by way of protection from the elements.

My father remembered the weather and one particularly bad winter when they were installing poles in wild barren country. This was an area of north Donegal near Carndonagh where you could travel for many a mile without encountering as much as a bush for shelter.

The truck would leave off a gang of men in the morning and the driver would be instructed to drive a mile further down the road in the evening when he returned to pick them up again. By that stage the men would have dug out about 15 holes and installed the poles and back filled each hole.

On many occasions as they worked in exposed locations with the lack of any form of shelter, the men would pour out their tea at lunchtime but as they drank out of the cup it never emptied – the rain just kept filling it up. These were fit hardy men who were not put off by weather conditions or the terrain that they had to carry poles through in order to get electricity to the remotest parts of the county.

These men were on a crusade, a job had to be done, a community had to be connected to electricity and they were most grateful for having the opportunity to do it.

He stated that as 'rural' developed over the years of the 1950s the hearts and minds of the people were finally won over. People soon realised the many benefits that the rural electrification scheme was rolling out. The convenience it afforded them compared to the old ways meant many came to embrace it with open arms.

My father spent 10 years working on 'rural' and it was the period of his working life that he got the most satisfaction from. I got the impression that this was largely due to the fact that he was part of a team of men who were the pioneers of their day. As he said himself there were was no need for leaders or bosses back then, every man was a leader and if one man was flagging there was always a colleague at hand to pick up the pieces and not let the side down.

Like most others involved in the rural electrification scheme my father has now sadly passed on also, but his small part in the rural electrification scheme in Donegal will remain.

God only knows what the consequences would have been if that man in that lorry on that day back in 1951 had not had second thoughts and not beckoned my father back and offered him a few weeks' work which lasted over 40 years. He died in 2007 aged 90 happy to have been part of the 'Rural' pioneers.

John McArt sat down with his father Pat shortly before he passed away to record the above account of his life within ESB. John, who is married with three children, is a native of Raphoe but has lived in Sligo for almost 40 years.

50

Shiny Promises
With Dad's Dodge
(Or Chrysler)
John Caffrey

IT wasn't just the seaside, or the swim, or even the promise of
ice cream, it was just being inside the big car itself.

Imagine suburban Cork life in the early 1950s, you'd be lucky
to see a second-hand Anglia or Ford Prefect. But who could imagine
a shiny, chrome-bedecked Chrysler or Dodge parked outside your
front door – even if it was just at weekends? That's how it was in our
house, all down to the Rural Electrification scheme.

My Dad worked as a driver with the newly-founded ESB. He was
a Dublin man and was proud of the various roles he held within that
organisation. Indeed, he dined out on the story of delivering the first
transformer to the Poulaphouca Reservoir, on the Kildare/Wicklow
border, and would tell all and sundry that he did so while driving one
of the first front wheel drive vehicles employed to perform such
monumental tasks.

I have a photograph of him from around this time and he is
sitting astride a motorbike. The machine has a sidecar complete with
passenger and the sidecar is emblazoned with the logo 'Electricity
Supply Board'.

He met and married my mother. She was a Cork woman, never
comfortable living in Dublin, so he transferred to Cork. However,
in so doing he discovered that he was similarly unhappy living in
Cork. But, back then, you stayed where the work was and got
along with life.

He worked from the depot in Albert Road, Cork, and I recall one

Saturday morning when I was about five years of age he brought me with him in the cab of a big red ESB lorry with a yellow zig-zag flash on the door.

We were delivering a small punt to the Inniscarra Dam for use by the Engineers. It was heady stuff for a small boy to witness!

My Dad's skills as a driver had not gone unnoticed within the ESB, and he was selected to chauffeur the new minor deities of the organisation, namely those same engineers, around Kerry and West Cork as the electrification programme was rolled-out.

He would dress up in collar and tie on a Monday morning and call to the train station to meet the Dublin-based, head-office arrivals. They would then embark upon travels about the region for the week, inspecting progress and planning the ongoing stages of the campaign. For the engineers this was massively responsible work and, accordingly, my Dad made sure that their journeys under his charge went as smoothly as possible. The car was always spick-and-span and he was forever punctual.

Each Friday he made sure that they were on time to catch the Dublin-bound train from Tralee or from Killarney. His work done for the week, he would then return home to us in Cork. We'd be waiting there for the big shiny car to show up outside the house. He'd always give a good long toot on the horn.

I recall that there was so much chrome-work on the car it would dazzle you to look too long upon it in full sunlight. Sometimes I'd look at my reflection in the bright work and see a distorted image, like you'd see in the funny mirrors at the amusement arcade.

Dad always had stories to tell when he got back from his exotic travels with the engineers. My mother would pump him for the lowdown on the various personalities of his passengers and what they had been up to during the week. I sat at the table fascinated at the goings-on of that major undertaking and so proud that my Dad was a big part of the important work.

The name Mr McLaughlin kept coming up during those mealtime conversations and, each time it did, was with such a degree of reverence. I imagined that he must surely be the most important man in the country.

Sundays were the big treat. If the weather was good he drove my two sisters, myself and my mother to the seaside at Crosshaven or Youghal. Somebody had to sit in the middle, but it never seemed to matter who got the place away from the window just as long as we were all together singing songs in that big shiny car.

There was the promise of ice cream if we were well-behaved and sandwiches and a flask of tea for the beach. When it came time to return home, my mother was careful to make sure that we cleaned all the sand from our sandals and there were dire warnings never to get sick in that back seat.

There were about two or three years of those big shiny cars before the job was finished and the engineers moved to another location allowing my Dad to go back to driving less remarkable vehicles.

I sometimes see one of those great big American cars on TV or in movies and think back to a time when the ESB engineers delivered light and made the wires sing around Cork and Kerry. It is unlikely though, that any of them ever knew that at they were also delivering the means for a small boy to receive the brightness of the seaside and to sing with his sisters in the back seat.

John Caffrey retired as chief laboratory technician from UCC in 2007 after working there for over 48 years. He has published many research papers on chromatography and organic water pollution. He holds an honorary masters degree in analytical chemistry.

"Still, looking back on it, things could have been much worse, at least my pump was intact in my trousers' pocket. I would live to love another day."

**Pearse O'Doherty –
'Who Stole The Flash Light?'**

51

Who Stole The Flash Light?

Pearse O'Doherty

IT was 1958 and a time when you wouldn't be safe leaving either a flash-light or a pump on your bike. There was a spate of thieving locally and it was not wise to take any chances.

However, in relation to the machines themselves, the amount of bicycles thrown up against one another and conjoined pedal to spoke like inseparable lovers was a sort of safety in numbers and you were fairly sure that yours would be still there whenever you exited the parochial hall dance.

There was excitement in our village near Longford, we were going to hear and see a new phenomenon, a showband. The Royal from Waterford were playing in the hall. The Parish Priest was none too pleased though. We were used to the Donal Ring Ceili Band or even the Clipper Carlton, but there was a reputation for hip-gyrating by the newcomers that was being frowned upon by certain well-placed members of the community. Electric guitars, microphones and amplifiers were a new phenomenon. The village was buzzing.

By the time I threw my bicycle into the tangle of similar machines up the lane and transferred the pump into the side pocket of my trousers, I could hear, as well feel, the bass notes vibrating beneath my feet as I crossed the street. There was a poster of the band, all decked out in matching shiny suits pasted to a lamp-post adjacent to the entrance. I paid my money into the biscuit tin at the table set up inside the door, went into the gents and queued up to take a turn in front of the mirror so as to straighten my tie and plaster down my hair with a sup of water.

I recall meeting up with a few of the lads down the end of the hall.

We were watching the dancers twirl past and commenting out of the corners of our mouths like convicts. I had my eye on a girl who was working at that time in the Post Office in town.

I was hoping she was present but couldn't see her anywhere. But then to my surprise, she walked past and smiled straight at me. I was so happy! I tried to arrange my face into something approximating a reciprocating smile, but was unsure of what I was doing.

She sat against the opposite wall and fell into conversation with a bunch of girls. The set ended and Tom Dunphy, the singer, spoke into the microphone declaring it was time for 'the next dance, please.'

It was time to make my move. I drifted onto the dance-floor and moved crablike towards my goal. It was a bit like tickling trout or lamping rabbits, you'd have to make it seem that you had no intention of being interested in the task in hand.

Timing was everything, but then disaster struck! Tom stepped up to the microphone, was announcing a slow set, when the lights went out. There were a few shrieks from the girls. I stood there, uncertain of what to do next. I kept going to where I thought I'd last seen the girl of my dreams and reached a hand to assure her in some manly fashion that all was ok.

Just then the lights flickered back on and the music struck up again. My hand was on the shoulder of the wrong girl, and what could I do but soldier on and start into the 'slow set' with the number two choice of dancing partner.

We were halfway through the first circuit of the dance floor when the lights blew again and the band went silent. This time it was for good. Matches burnt down in calloused fingers as experts in electrical matters tried to fix the fault.

But it was no use, the demand on the simple electrics of the Parochial Hall was too much. It turned out that there were just a couple of overloaded sockets burdened with the amplification of the showband.

The man in charge of the biscuit tin offered a refund as we trooped out the door, disappointed in love and in life. The girl in the Post Office moved to a bigger town a short time afterwards and I never saw her again.

It was a long while before the electrics of the Parochial Hall were upgraded to a standard sufficient to power the amplification of the likes of The Royal Showband. They remained as they had been when they were installed in those very early days of the Rural Electrification scheme.

However there was one further frustration to that infamous night, when I returned to collect my bicycle, someone had stolen my flash-lamp. Still, looking back on it, things could have been much worse, at least my pump was intact in my trousers' pocket. I would live to love another day.

Pearse O'Doherty is a fiddle player and expert fly-fisherman. He has lived most of his life in County Longford.

"As things turned out neither Mary Jo nor John were to know that the 'electric light' coming to their village would change the course of their lives in more ways than one."

T.J. Byrne – 'Of Love And Loss'

52

Of Love And Loss

T.J. Byrne

MARY JO was 17 and was regarded as the best looking girl in the locality with her flaxen hair and blue eyes. She was working part-time in the local co-op which was about five miles away.

She cycled into town in the mornings having helped to get her younger brothers and sisters out to school as her mother had died five years earlier. She was the eldest of a big family and was very bright having done well in her Intermediate Cert the previous year.

Mary Jo was ambitious and was expected to do well in her job, as well as any working class girl could expect to do at that time. She had a boyfriend for about a year, a local lad by the name of John who also worked as an apprentice shop boy in town.

They were inseparable and went everywhere together. Everyone said that they were lovely youngsters and would make a grand couple when they were a bit older. All was going well with Mary Jo in work and in love when things took on a turn with the arrival of the ESB linesmen in the village for the Rural Electrification Scheme.

There was an influx of linesmen and other skilled men who had qualifications from other counties. Some of the men stayed in digs and farmers houses in the area and they were a sort of novelty with everyone talking about them.

The younger ones cut quite a dash with the local women, none more so than one by the name of Sandy. He had good looks, fancy clothes, a slick haircut and a big red motorbike.

John noticed that since their arrival in town, Mary Jo began to make excuses and didn't want to go out in the evenings. He made enquiries and found out that she had been seen in the company of one of the 'electric light' crew.

He went to her house and confronted her straight away and she admitted that she had been seeing the linesman with the red hair. She felt a bit guilty about the whole thing as she knew John cared a lot for her and he was, after all, her first boyfriend. But guilt or no guilt things had moved on and there was no going back. She was living in a dream world and really enjoying it.

Sandy was working on those big transformers that were being put up on the poles, he was an electrician and he had the papers to show it. He brought her for drives on the back of his BSA motorbike, going to the pictures and the dances in the surrounding towns; to the seaside at Brittas Bay and Arklow and he even brought her to the Spring Show in Ballsbridge. In short, Sandy swept her off her feet and she didn't have a chance to hold back.

As things turned out neither Mary Jo nor John were to know that the 'electric light' coming to their village would change the course of their lives in more ways than one. A short time later she found out that she was pregnant and didn't know where or who to turn to for help.

When she met Sandy a couple of evenings later she blurted out the news. He turned white with shock. He panicked, said it couldn't be him and besides he had a girlfriend at home. Mary Jo knew then she was on her own.

She had no mother to talk to and her sisters were too young to understand. She couldn't tell her father as he wouldn't understand how she got herself into such a situation.

In desperation she remembered that a distant relative of the family had been ordained to the priesthood a couple of years earlier. As it happened he was home on holiday and Mary Jo plucked up the courage to confide in him. He was very understanding and sympathetic to her plight. Nevertheless he knew where the parish priest stood on such matters and had no option but to advise her to go to him and to take someone along with her. Mary Jo approached her Aunt Maisie and told her the story.

Aunt Maisie was good-living but also a woman of the time who believed in the Catholic Church and its teachings. However, she agreed to accompany Mary Jo to see the parish priest, Fr. Ryan.

He was very hard-line on all things to do with sex and morals and after questioning Mary Jo at length, he informed her she would have to go to a home. He said that she should come back to him within the week when he would have arranged a place for her.

Maisie broke the news to Mary Jo's father, Paddy, who took it rather badly. He was angry with Mary Jo but had enough humanity to know that anything he said would only add to her misery. He went to see the priest but Fr. Ryan gave him short shrift. All he said is that he would let him know when he should bring the girl and her belongings to the parochial house for the journey to a convent across the midlands.

A few days later, Paddy and Maisie brought Mary Jo to the parochial house with her small suitcase. Fr Lynch, the curate, had the car ready and they set off for the convent in the midlands. Paddy sat in the front with the priest while Mary Jo sat in the back with Maisie.

Mary Jo was scared and struggled to hold back the tears on the long journey. She had never spent a night out of her own house before this and didn't know what to expect as no one had bothered to tell her what was going on.

A small little nun brought Mary Jo into a reception room where she took her details and got Paddy to sign that he was handing the girl over. She then escorted her to her dormitory where there was a long line of tiny steel beds with girls already asleep in them.

The next morning she met the others washing at a line of basins filled with cold water on the dormitory. She knew that they were all there for the same reason.

Mary Jo cried herself to sleep every night for that first two weeks in the convent. Gradually she got to know a few of the girls who were friendly; they helped her with her work when she didn't feel well.

While the work was hard Mary Jo didn't mind as she was well used to it. What she found harder to deal with was the scolding and the attitude of some of the nuns.

After getting Mary Jo sorted, Fr Ryan turned his attentions to Sandy. He went to his district supervisor and demanded that he be sacked from his job and banished from the parish. The supervisor said that he could not do that as there were rules he would have to follow but Fr. Ryan reminded him in no uncertain terms that the ESB owed him a favour.

In the end the supervisor agreed to move Sandy to another district where he would not have any contact with anyone from the area, particularly the single girls of the parish.

Mary Jo was five months in the convent when her baby daughter was born on a Sunday morning. She was only allowed to hold the baby for about an hour before being forced to give her up for adoption.

When she left the convent, Mary Jo got a job in a nearby town as she knew she could not go back to her own place. Fortunately, she met a young man called Pat within a matter of months who treated her well and within a year they got married and ended up having a large family.

Mary Jo kept in touch with a few of her old neighbours over the years and they said that she carried no resentment about her treatment by the clergy who were supposed to be showing mercy.

She had long ago forgiven them for depriving her of her liberty and above all for depriving her of her daughter. Fr. Ryan was a product of his time and training and was part of a Church that had an obsession with the sexual mores of their flock.

I believe Mary Jo never spoke of Sandy in later years but I know she did resent the fact that he left her on her own at a very vulnerable time. In later years when these thing began to be discussed more openly, Mary Jo made efforts to trace her daughter but came up against bureaucracy at every turn and the only lead that she got was that she had been adopted by an English couple. However she still hoped to make contact and meet with her someday but sadly it never happened.

Mary Jo passed away recently and a few of her old neighbours travelled to the funeral in her adopted town where we met her sons and daughters and their families.

It did my heart good to see that this fine lady – who had to leave her first home under a cloud of embarrassment – was surrounded by such genuine people as she prepared to journey to her final resting place.

T.J. Byrne now lives in Carlow, is a part time farmer and writes in his spare time.

53

Wary Of Fairies' Wrath Along The Zig-zag Line

Joe Keane

FOR weeks, even months, the rumours had spread around the parish like Chivers marmalade; in the shops and after Sunday Mass little else was the main topic of conversation. The postman – Reuter's News Agency on wheels in those days – confirmed that our area would be next.

"They have finished in Roscommon, so they will be here next week," he informed the faithful.

Like many such events, when it did happen it was almost an anti-climax. One morning in 1954, the Rural Electrification crew descended on our townland like paratroopers landing behind enemy lines.

They moved silently, stacking electric poles strategically in carefully planned locations throughout the district. This whirlwind of activity soon overwhelmed all, both beast and human.

Over the following weeks they cratered the fields and knocked lumps of plaster as big as clamps of turf out of concrete walls. Those boys meant business. Very soon they were making major advances towards Gurteen and other important locations like Monasteraden and Cloonloo.

There are none as innovative as young people when it comes to inventiveness. Give a girl silk thread and a needle and she will fashion a pretty embroidery. If a boy has two polish tins and a piece of string he will improvise a telephone. The ESB with its array of curious accessories, like transformers and cables, produced the ideal fodder to fuel the young imagination.

Back then, ESB officials had to act with great tact when dealing with delicate local issues. Digging near lios's and raths for example, was considered no-go areas by many of the older people.

In South Sligo we were at some remove from the whispering woods of Lisadell and the quiet serenity of Ben Bulben. But we were not completely bereft of the Yeatsian magic and charm. We too had our fairies and goblins. One elderly man was incensed when the ESB tried to erect poles in one particular part of his property.

The man had sometime before suffered a supernatural experience. He was milking his cows outdoors one summer evening. This was a practice at the time. The unfortunate man was seized by a condition called the 'Fa' – a form of temporary disorientation. He walked about in a daze for several hours and ended up in unfamiliar countryside. He was convinced that he had in some way incurred the wrath of the fairies; and now he was not about to do so again.

But the ESB's skills of diplomacy once again proved effective and a difficult crisis was averted in the end.

The mix of workers recruited for the Rural Electrification Scheme threw up many interesting contrasts. Old Harney (I never knew his first name) was a small lithe man. His well-deserved reputation as a good worker was known far and near. On the bog, his turf cutting prowess was legendary, feeding two 'spreader's' at a time, as he quickly demolished the turf banks.

"Would he adapt well to the new conditions of digging for poles?" the cynics queried. They did not need to be concerned. The criterion employed in those days was that a worker was expected to dig three triangular holes per day. Whizz-kids at the time considered that the equilateral triangle, allowed sufficient space to yield a shovel (or pick) for the digger, as he excavated deeper.

In 'old Harney's' case he normally disposed of four or even five such holes, much to the chagrin of his fellow worker.

Then there was Tom. Now his was a different example of the able bodied labourer. He was interested in work alright and could watch people toiling all day. He belonged to that set of drinkers (of which we all had a nodding acquaintance) who would consider drinking eight pints just the start of a session.

Like most young men in the locality, he found himself caught up in the wave of employment that was becoming available. On his very first day at work, he had not gone down far in the hole, when he encountered a large boulder. No matter how much coaxing or cajoling he exerted, it remained jammed. Finally he sought help from fellow workers. After a long time the errant rock was hauled to the surface.

At that moment the man of the house looked out the door. When he saw Tom, his old drinking pal, he rushed over and put out his hand.

"How are ya Tom?" he exclaimed. "Yer welcome to our townland."

At that moment, the rock slipped back into the hole again. The man cleared off quickly leaving the pair to undergo the whole process once more.

Many farmers houses used whistles in those times. When the men were working in a distant field, the housewife called them in for the dinner (midday meal) by this means.

My pal Jerry and I noticed that when the engineers were plotting the lines, they used whistles as a means of contacting each other. Evidently they had devised a code of some kind.

We concealed ourselves in a nearby ditch and produced whistling sounds similar to theirs. After a while there was a predictable outcome as our whistling interruptions meant plotted lines were formed in a zig-zag pattern. We were soon discovered and routed from our hiding place.

Joe Keane lives with his wife in Co Mayo and since retiring has taken up creative writing as a hobby. A number of his stories have been published.

"He was barred from two of the three local pubs and was always one fight away from being barred from the only other one. Batt could be grumpy but he was a genius who was a self-taught engineer."

**Gerry Tuohey –
'It Takes A Village To Raise A Child!'**

54

It Takes A Village To Raise A Child!

Gerry Tuohy

S a child growing up in a little village in Wicklow, I was blessed to have as my playground a hill, a mountain, a fairy fort and a river that went from a trickling brook in summer to a raging waterway in winter.

Many's the summer day I hung over the bank of that river waiting and hoping to catch the sly pinkeens that seldom showed. I'd stay until the midges began to eat me alive.

Many's the winter night I found myself caught out too late in darkness, and not wanting to travel the mile to the bridge, try to manoeuvre my way across the torrent by negotiating the tips of submerged boulders. My parents were at home blissfully unaware of my death defying antics.

So much happens in a child's life that goes unreported. Like the raft incident. The river was in spate and a group of us found abandoned barrels. We thought we'd bind the barrels together with rope and take on the rapids.

Holding the raft against the bank became impossible, so we all dived aboard together for fear of being the one left behind. The panicked boarding caused a pendulum effect which put us into a tailspin.

We lost one lad as we overcorrected the weight imbalance. The raft raised into the air and crashed back into the river. The ropes held for at least two smashes before the lot unravelled sending the whole crew tumbling into the brown river.

We went home like drowned rats.

Darkness was the norm at that time, we did homework by

candlelight that waved and dodged across our books at the whim of any breeze sailing through the house. We were all excited when we heard talk of arrival of a new phenomenon.

Electricity crews were everywhere to be seen. Machinery and materials were in fields and along the roads. Some were very wary about the new phenomenon. One such person was 'Batt the Lift.'

He was barred from two of the three local pubs, and was always one fight away from being barred from the only other one. Batt could be grumpy but he was a genius who was a self-taught engineer.

There wasn't house or farm in the parish that he had not designed some gadget or other for. He made mill wheels, hand-carved from Wicklow granite. He made potato spinners and ploughs, big and small from the left over steel in an abandoned factory back the road. He was known as 'Batt the lift', as he had designed and made his very own hoist that consisted of a gearbox comprising of a series of toothed gears that were driven by pulling on a looped chain. These gears, when rotated, turned another set of gears which in turn pulled on a much bigger chain. This larger chain had a hook on the end of it which would be connected to whatever item that needed to be lifted up.

With the engineering of the gears it was possible to, with very little effort, lift a very heavy weight. To me this was magical. On many occasions I lifted engines and ploughs that were many times my weight.

I remember one day standing beside Bat and talking to him about the Rural Electrification. He turned on me and said: "I grew up in the dark an' I don't want any bloody electricity."

It came over the fields through Mulligan's farm, and stopped at the top road beside the gate to our top field. Batt ranted: "Johnny Mulligan let the 'electric' in all over his farm and even my cattle know something's not right. You can hear them bawlin' if they go near the boundary ditch. No good will ever come of it. Cattle sense things."

When the crews were in the village, Batt was extremely vigilant. He watched everything from his yard. When electricity officials called to his gate he would run them.

On a couple of occasions, I recall seeing him just standing and looking back towards the bridge in the dead of night.

My dad didn't want the electricity either but my mam persuaded him to sign up. The day they put up the poles on our farm dad was back the road turning hay. When he came home mam told him the electricity would be here shortly. She brought me up to Mulligans to see how it worked. Mr Mulligan was like the 'cat that got the cream' because he 'stole a march' on a lot of the parish by getting the electricity straight away.

When we walked into his yard he was standing there with his wife. Daylight had just turned and I could just make out his dog crouching in the corner of the yard. The next thing Mulligan reached into the porch and did something. I will never forget the fright I got when his yard went white with brilliance. It was brighter that November night than a sunny afternoon in June. I could see the dog clear as day – with pups sitting beside it. His wife must have seen the fright I got because she took my hand and brought me into their kitchen.

The kitchen was in darkness. The next thing Mrs Mulligan said 'watch your eyes' and she pushed down a switch on the wall. I was so frightened that I pushed past mam out into the yard and sat outside waiting for her, in the darkness.

In our house, I was fascinated by this big lad with a broad smile and an even broader Dublin accent who came to do the wiring. He explained everything he did from mounting the cable on the wall, to connecting the allocated two sockets. He talked me through the wiring to the new fuse box and he told my mam that I was to be the technical representative of the house, which made so proud, I was fit to burst.

Some while later during the harvesting of potatoes in the river field, our spinning machine got tangled up with steel wire that was thrown amongst the drills. Everything came to a halt as the wire tightened itself with each revolution.

A visit to 'Batt the lift' was required. When we pulled into his yard, he directed us to the rear of the haybarn. Here stood in all its glory, Batt's newly-constructed towering hoist. Reaching 15 feet into the air in a wigwam formation, were three freshly creosoted electricity poles with the hoist suspended from the centre of them.

Those poles had been up in a ditch on the main road not two weeks previously and had been the topic of discussion amongst the neighbours since their disappearance.

Batt looked at my dad and then included me into the conspiracy by means of a slow wink. "I knew some good would come out of that electric nonsense. I just had to wait me chance, that was all."

You could argue though that the ESB had the last laugh. Before long, electric motors were lifting weights across the nation at a rate that 'Batt the lift' could only dream of.

Gerry Tuohy is a sports enthusiast, writer and storyteller who lives in Wicklow.

55

When In Doubt, Stop Digging

Tom Breen

WELL now, who is it that once said the path of true love never ran smooth? Indeed the ESB, or 'the electric', as it was better known back then, added its own unique spark to that particular saying.

Why don't you hush away the dog off the chair and push up 'till I explain what I mean.? You see my grandfather, Patrick Hayes, or Patie Hayes, as he was more affectionately known, was the County Civil Engineer for Limerick north, south, east and west of the county.

He yielded as much political weight as the 20-odd stone that he carried about his waist. A man who preferred to be unchallenged, what he said was law and he made no apology for it. He was held in high esteem because, bear in mind, for the most part, local people were illiterate. That might explain the line of men and women at his hall door most evenings asking him to read letters they had received from England and America and to perhaps give advice on trespassing cattle and all classes of other minor disputes and points of law.

It was no surprise to any that this forward-looking gentleman was the first around the area to have the electric installed. His wife died young in childbirth and my mother took over the role of secretary and housekeeper for Patie. She enjoyed all the benefits that electricity brought to her life in that house.

But, when my mother married a man from 12 miles away, storm clouds gathered in her life. On arrival in her new home she was thrown backwards into the world of paraffin and wicks and candles.

As an automatic reflex, she continually placed her hand up to turn on the electric light switch whenever she entered the darkened house, but there was nothing for her to touch except the blank cold wall. She would have to endure the loss of comfort for a full three years.

But my father, being a man of honour, would tackle up the pony and trap every Sunday and take her back to her family home so that she could hit the switch and watch the electric light illuminate the darkness. There was no word in the local lexicon back then that equated to what we might call 'divorce' but if there was, I'm sure she might have contemplated it. However, in the nick of time, the ESB arrived to save a marriage and one woman's sanity!

There were other local, minor dramas recorded around this time. There is a common belief in our area of Athlacca that the best bread ever baked was that produced by Tim the Baker. But around the time of Rural Electrification, the man surrendered his skill with dough and flour and instead enlisted with the ESB digging holes for poles.

(When challenged as to why he turned his back on feeding the community, he'd suggest that the ESB offered him 'real' money and not the barter system that he had to contend with up to then.)

Tim was never short of the loan of a horse to plough his half-acre or a bucket of milk for the bakery but he was often left wanting relative to hard currency. But when he saw a chance to dig a hole a day for a pole a day and get paid for his efforts, he said it was a solution to his personal economic war.

Another local man Philly, like Tim, cycled miles each day to join the pole digging crews. A 30-mile round trip was nothing to him. He was not a tall man. When challenged as to his height, he'd say that he was either 4ft 6 or 4ft 7 depending on which end of the ruler you held! When Philly was digging, the ganger was known to shout: " I know you are not six feet down yet Philly, I can still see the top of your head."

Tadhg was from the Hill. He was known to be well-versed, well-read and well-travelled. His mother came from humble beginnings in Kilmallock. She worked as a maid in the priest's house and went on to marry the sacristan. The Good Lord blessed them with one son, Tadhg. This mother made sure that he was given every opportunity in life. She ensured that he could read and write. Most of all she wanted him to get out there travel and see the great world. He eventually fulfilled her ambition by getting a job as a bus conductor in Dublin.

Now you most likely wonder what this has to do with electricity or Rural Electrification? Everyone locally looked forward to Tadhg's thrice yearly return home from the big city so that they could get all the news from abroad.

As luck would have it, didn't Tadhg meet a man who claimed to be an electrical engineer as a passenger on one particular bus journey. This man told him that he had a great money-saving tip for those contemplating getting in the light.

He explained that what consumers should do was use the same bulb in each room. For example, illuminate the kitchen bulb and then when it had heated up remove it from the bulb-holder and quickly transfer it to the next room to be lit up. His idea was that by using the same bulb it would be broken-in, so to speak, and therefore be hot from the previous room. This, in turn, would spare the current and reduce the cost.

Tadhg the Hill was delighted to pass on his new-found knowledge the next time he returned home. It is still remembered locally how his conservation tip had half the local women driven mad from climbing onto chairs and nearly killing themselves screwing in hot bulbs in the complete darkness.

It was a trend that never fully caught on around Athlacca.

Tom Breen is from Athlacca in Co Limerick. He is a storyteller, historian and gatherer of folklore.

"It was also the dawning of environmental awareness in the country and voices were heard from conservationists about the possible adverse environmental impact this work could leave in such an unspoilt area."

Michael Daly – 'The Black Valley – Last Piece Of Jigsaw'

56

The Black Valley –
Last Piece Of Jigsaw
Michael Daly

T HE Black Valley near Beaufort in County Kerry was really the last piece in the big rural electrification scheme jigsaw. A place of tremendous scenic beauty, it is a very sparsely populated area that still had no electricity long after Ireland had joined the then EEC in the early 1970s.

It was passed over in the earlier schemes that had gone around the county because it didn't qualify on a cost benefit analysis.

In fact, it probably would have met the criterion required under these headings but with an election not a million miles away in 1976, the Coalition Government of the time took the decision to do something.

Corkman Peter Barry was the Minister for Transport and Power and it was through his office that The Black Valley Bill came before and was passed through Dail Eireann. This allowed rural electricity to be brought not just to the Black Valley but all isolated homes across Ireland who through an accident of geography had not, until that time, enjoyed the 'miracle' of electricity.

The Black Valley was always going to be difficult to electrify because not only was it thinly populated and remote, the ground was extremely boggy, making it far from ideal for timber poles to be placed firmly in the ground. This added considerably to the cost. As the engineer in charge I remember that electrifying the valley involved standing 400 poles into the ground to bring supplies to 39 homes.

It was because of its remoteness and the fact that it had been passed over so many times that around 1976 the plight of people living in the dark ages in The Black Valley caught the public imagination.

There was a series of articles in newspapers and magazines, all of which thought this was indeed a sad situation considering the other advances that had come to the country. It was also the dawning of environmental awareness in the country and voices were heard from conservationists about the possible adverse environmental impact this work could leave in such an unspoilt area.

The pragmatists' voices were stronger in that era and those championing the cause of welcoming 'the light' into the valley won out, with certain reservations. Kerry's chief planning officer John McElligott took a personal interest in the scheme and specified that no oak trees were to be cut down though he conceded that they could be trimmed.

We decided to help the aesthetics of the area in any way we could. Where possible, we kept poles away from view along main roads or tourist hotspots. I think we did OK in this regard because at the end of the installation to the Valley, the Irish Times remarked that we had done "a remarkable job" in sensitively siting the poles.

The young people welcomed the electricity because it meant they could watch television and do their homework in proper light. By contrast their mothers finally got to experience the creature comforts such as washing machines and fridges that the first beneficiaries of the scheme had enjoyed for 30 years.

The farmers too entered the modern time by having the advantage of pumped water into house and farmyard. And for the first time, they heard the hum of the milking machine in the byre.

In a programme to celebrate the silver anniversary of the coming of light to the Black Valley in 2002, one resident Eugene Tangney, while warmly welcoming the advent of electricity, also lamented the loss of cards games and story telling from the district.

The big losers of 1977, of course, were the coalition government parties, on whose watch the work had been done. Jack Lynch's resurgent Fianna Fail routed Fine Gael and Labour.

One woman from the Black Valley said she was sorry for Peter Barry after he had got the light for them...but added that she was glad the 'Cruiser' (Conor Cruise O'Brien) had lost his seat.

Michael Daly is a former ESB engineer who was in charge of the Black Valley installation. A native of Kiskeam, Co Cork, he now lives near Blarney.

57

Ireland From The Half-way House

PJ Cunningham

I GREW up in the half-way house period of our history when Ireland was starting to move forward after the stagnation following independence – often on unsure feet.

The fifties and sixties saw the fledgling nation welcoming modern ways. This adaptation across virtually every strata of society would as the decades passed turn Ireland into a first world country, albeit with the odd almighty fall back to our knees as a reminder of where we came from.

My mother's birthplace was a thatched cottage a mile from the nearest town. By the time I could reach a switch on the wall, my aunt and uncle who lived in the house with their young family, had married the traditional ways of lighting to the new in an economic accommodation that they saw as giving the best of both worlds.

The kitchen and big bedroom had single naked bulbs installed but the dairy and parlour areas of the house were lit by candle or lamp only. This was the solution for many families when it came to installing power and light under the Rural Electrification scheme without exposing themselves too much to the risk of cost.

Usually a local man prepared the wiring that was later subject to inspection by ESB or their agents. His work was passed by the higher authorities and in every way was fine except when he later returned after a water accident, he inadvertently put the light switch in the kitchen upside down at the kitchen door.

It was his only known aberration, unlike the man I've since heard about who did all the local wiring in a town in neighbouring Co

Laois. His unfortunate trademark was every light switch he ever did was the wrong way around.

In the case of my aunt's house it was only when the man had finished the repair work that he realised what he had done. To his eternal credit, he called the family together in the kitchen to tell them that they should always remember that 'up' was 'on' in the kitchen and 'down' was off.

We remembered it well for the rest of our lives but unfortunately he didn't. Some years later following another leak in the thatched roof – and this was believed to be the reason the light wouldn't go on – he was sent for to see if he could restore the power.

The man was both gentle and good-humoured which meant a lot to children eagerly watching his every working move. He did his usual tracing of where the problem might be sourced by checking wires but was unable to find a solution.

In desperation, he climbed onto a chair, took the bulb out of the overhead pendant and as in the days before phase testers, he automatically turned his eyes over in the direction of the switch on the wall.

It was in the 'up' position so he proceeded with his work around the bulb happy that he was safe to do so. There was no danger until he stuck a finger up in the place where the bulb meets its holder – which was live.

In the moment of contact, his eyes bulged, his hair stood on his head and he jumped off the chair all in one shrieking movement.

In that instant we thought we were witnessing the first electrocution of the Rural Electrification scheme.

However the man recovered his poise almost immediately, albeit a little less sure of his bearings than before he got the electric shot into his system. Our eyes were out of our heads looking on; he smiled at us before graciously recalling: "Ah, I should have known, sure this is the kitchen where 'up' is 'down'".

Over the years as I recall this moment, I think his was the perfect example of someone suffering a 'hoist with his own petard', though unlike Shakespeare, this man's intention was never to hurt other people.

Our youth was straddled in this halfway existence between the candle and the 60-Watt bulb – 100 Watts were banned in the houses of most small holdings as a perceived financial necessity.

The new progress in Irish life was welcomed because of the new comforts and labour savings it brought in its slipstream.

At home, I spent half my early years getting out of a warm bed at night to turn off the light before going to sleep. But it didn't compare to the experience of going to bed to the flicker of a candle flame in my aunt's house.

The lesser light from a flame turned my cousin's bedroom into a cinema where walls and presses and pictures and mirrors were transformed in the suggestion of the half-light. It mystically mutated a plain cottage room into a chamber of all possibilities.

The nights that I didn't stay under that roof, my uncle brought me home on what he made a mesmeric mile journey to our own house.

He was a man who was modern enough to have a tractor before most around our area owned one but he had the heart of an academic if not a poet. Which was why in those walks, he never saw the dark in front of him because his head was forever scanning the sky above.

At the crossroads at the head of the hill, we seldom passed without stopping to meander across the heavens from the Bear to the Plough with the constant Northern star always getting honourable mention among the constellations.

It was as if he got the Milky Way to flow down to this hilly country road as he interpreted the mysteries of other orbits for a little boy experiencing new worlds and new concepts of being.

"We know nothing about light down here," he said one night as we both witnessed a falling star.

Folklore had it, he explained, that such an occurrence was the sign of a soul going into heaven.

However he had more a scientific than a superstitious mind. "The real mystery is that star we saw had travelled millions of miles before we could see it."

Of course at seven or eight, I could only take on so much of his interpretations but some still remain etched in my memory. "Find me the North Star and I can take you anywhere," he'd say.

He unveiled night in all its mystery; when others brought me home, it was a case of getting to our front door as quickly as possible. My uncle opened a wonderland of sight and sound under the umbrella of the night sky that I've not looked up at long enough since to know if it still exists.

Back then in that little winding road one mile long, only six lights shone from the different dwellings as we sauntered our way between homes.

"This will all change," he predicted. "It's called the march of time."

He foresaw the advent of power to farmyards under the Rural Electrification Scheme as a sort of industrialisation of agriculture.

"None of ye or our young ones will ever farm for a living like us," he addressed me as if he was talking to an adult.

"And, you know, you'd be bigger eejits if you even thought of doing it," he added.

PJ Cunningham is an author, editor, publisher and journalist. A native of Clara, Co Offaly, he is married with five grown up children and now lives in Bray, Co Wicklow.

POEMS
& SONGS
FROM RURAL ELECTRIFICATION

Why I Wrote The Poem 'Changing Light'

Phil Lynch

THE poem 'Changing Light' recalls one of my earliest memories and still one of the most socially significant things to have happened in my lifetime, namely, the arrival of electricity to my childhood home in the north midlands under the rural electrification scheme.

The work had been going on in the area for some time until one particular day the crew arrived to make the final connection from the network to the house. My father was unaware that the supply was now live and the rest of us set up a ruse to surprise him.

The plan was to not light the Tilley lamp that evening as usual so that when he came in from work as it was getting dark he would want to know why there was no lamp lighting and probably set about lighting it himself. The plan worked to perfection. If anything, he was a bit later than usual coming into the house so that it was darker than we'd even expected.

Sure enough, he was surprised and, if the truth be told, slightly annoyed that nobody had lit the lamp. It was at this point that we activated the rest of the plan.

I, as the youngest, had been designated to 'throw the switch'. As soon as my mother gave the signal, I flicked the switch and the whole place lit up with the light from the electric bulb hanging from the ceiling. My father, and indeed the rest of us, were initially stunned by the suddenness and intensity of the illumination which gave way in a few seconds to a sense of joy that electricity had finally arrived and excitement at the prospects it offered into the future for our way of living.

In a wider context, it was in the era when western (cowboy) movies held sway and the cold war was in full swing and the poem includes certain references and terminology relating to both.

CHANGING LIGHT

It was nearly dark
when he came in from the fields
tired from the toils of the day
ready to complain
about the Tilley lamp still unlit,
would he have to light it himself
he asked of no one in particular.
In the shadow of an empty space
beneath the stairs
I stood primed.
The men with the metal boots,
their belts heavy as a gunslinger's,
had spent what seemed like years
digging holes to plant the creosote forest
that stretched across the countryside,
with giant spools of wire unfurled
along roads and lanes and fields.
I marvelled at how they scaled
the heights of those black poles
and worked at right angles to the ground
without falling,
stuntmen all.
In the countdown to dusk I waited
finger on the switch
as if to take its pulse
or like some general in the Kremlin
with his thumb on the red button
waiting for the order to push.
The pre-determined signal came
from my mother at the table
and with all the strength
in my bony digit
I flicked the magic switch.
Outside, the dusk turned instantly to dark.
Inside, the light would never be the same.

Phil Lynch lives in Dublin and is a multi-award winning poet and writer who is Co-Director of the Lingo Literary Festival. The above poem is contained in the recent anthology from the publishers Salmon Poetry. A version of the poem was also a commended runner-up in the Yeats Poetry Competition in 2014.

Measuring The Poles
Moira Gallagher

Poles and wires spreading over the countryside
Heralding great changes to come
No more need for oil lamps or candles
The new light would be bright as the sun.
My grand uncle Patrick sat listening
Turning the news over in his mind.
Caught up in the excitement all around him
While electric light he wouldn't see – he was blind.
On his daily walk I'd take his hand
And lead him where he wanted to go.
I'd count the animals in each field for him
And changes in crops he wanted to know.
He knew each landmark on the road
Each bend and rise, each gate and lane.
And every day, by the Blackland gate
The stopping place, always the same.
"Open the gate lass, we'll step inside,
There's something I must see."
We'd carefully tread over the rutted ground
The old man hanging on to me.
Slowly edging across with stumbling steps
To where the poles were piled, lying in wait
For the crew from the E.S.B. to come
And line them up at a later date.
My grand uncle then my hand let go
And commenced the daily routine.
In cubits the length was measured out
His hands, compensating for sight unseen.
Was he trying to work out the relationship
Between this wood and the new power to be?
As if fleshing the bones of what he had heard

About this great phenomenon, the E.S.B.
My grand uncle never experienced
The joy of light at the flick of a switch
But from his world of darkness and shadows
His light shone from within, deep and rich.
And I was fortunate and lucky
To learn from this frail blind man
Patience, inquisitiveness and wonder
Making of life the very best you can.

Moira Gallagher is a native of Creeslough but now lives in Lifford, Co Donegal. She is a retired teacher who writes stories and poems as a hobby.

A Nod From The Boss

Bunty Flynn

The meeting was held,
The hall was full up
Such a difference, such a difference
All the wise men said
BUT it's not natural my grandmother said,
She was the BOSS and what she said went.
It could burn the house down and kill us in our beds,
I won't let it inside the door,
Too dangerous, she said
But Missus, at the flick of a switch
You will have light all around
It's clean and it's safe, it's the modern thing
It's fast and it's cheap: my father said
It could set fire to the thatch
Then what would we do
On the side of the road we'd be
Because of you and your light
But the wires are insulated
It's perfectly safe
And you can boil a kettle by plugging it in
You'd have tea in your hand in five minutes flat
My grandmother said:
I'd doubt that
And a gleaming white cooker with no turf or smoke,
Would boil the spuds and make the bacon and cabbage sing
And all at the same time, so fast and so clean,
An electric cooker would be a wonderful thing
And what would I do with all that time saved?

Sure I'm sitting here with one leg in the grave
In the event of a wake, my aunt piped up
The house would be neat as a pin
Cause you could plug in a machine that would suck up the dirt
And the old goose wing would be left in the lurch

And the sheets and the blankets
No need to scrub
A machine would do it
It's called a twin tub
You could sew on your machine
Till well into the night
No need for lamps and paraffin oil,
Tilly lamps and candle grease would be a thing of the past
Go on out of that
Sure 'tis too good to be true
You'll be telling me next
It could milk a cow
Oh, yes indeed,
That's an amazing fact
It can do just that and milk a few at the time
 was my uncle's retort
Holding up her hand
My grandmother said: STOP
And what about God?
It was he who said, "Let there be light"
He is the man in charge of us all, don't you forget.
But, you say it comes on a wire? How's that?
Yes, on poles brought in from abroad
Each house will be wired from here to the coast
A rosary of poles to bring us the light
But only to us if we sign up Monday night
You are talking me into it, I know what you're at
She said, cocking her head sideways and tugging her hat
Gosh! My mother said, sure I almost forgot
There would be no need for a candle or a paraffin lamp:

A Nod From The Boss

All day and all night a little red bulb
would glow in front of the Sacred Heart.
And so she said: YES. My grandmother boss
And signed her name with a shake of her head
But 'till the day she died she wore her kid gloves
When plugging in the kettle for her morning cup
One can't be too careful.
My grandmother said.

*Bunty Flynn is a retired playschool teacher who lives in Mitchelstown,
Co Cork. Married with three children and is a member of a Writer's
Group.*

Rural Electrification
Michael Lynch

I'm happy to say, that in some small way,
I've done something for this generation.
For long long ago, I worked on a scheme,
Called the Rural Electrification.
With shovel and spade, no mechanical aid,
Not a word about mechanization.
I dug many holes, climbed thousands of poles,
On the Rural Electrification.
I loved that ould job, I earned many's a bob,
And I travelled to every location,
And like many's another, I found my good wife,
On the Rural Electrification.
You can now have a shower, with ESB power,
And for news keep in touch with the nation,
And you won't need a bucket, to go to the well,
With Rural Electrification.

*Michael Lynch is a former long-standing ESB official from Co Cavan.
He is married with eight grown-up children and enjoys writing as a
hobby*

On Christmas Morning

Noel King

My father's father is bounding across his farm.
Three small heads follow, having brought the gifts
Of the Magi to less fortunates, short-cutted by their own fields.
The patriarch ignores the bulk of poles
The country has erected on his land,
Though he is grateful for the electric in his home.
Santa Claus was able to turn on the kitchen light
And see where everything went last night;
Coming to the younger ones: a boy trotting here now,
And a girl at home with mother making Christmas.
Outside this morning, after presents, and looking skywards,
The children sent a prayer to take him safe to the North Pole.
This evening all will milk cows and break bread
Into little pieces for birds in the cold.
But the family will go to Mass next
Where children will whisper
Of the wonders of the man in the red suit.
My father's mother will raise the window sash
Any moment now and her husband will see again
Across a love grown in them.
She will call a greeting, wave
And years away their children will remember Christmas.

Noel King was born and lives in Tralee, Co Kerry. In this his 50th year, he has reached his 1,000th publication of a poem, haiku or short story in magazines and journals in 38 countries. A short story collection, The Key Signature & Other Stories will be published by Liberties Press in 2017.

The ESB

Danny Sullivan na Ceapacha
(Slightly abridged version of the song)

Oh Johnny dear and did you hear what all the neighbours say
That the ESB with electricity have landed in Coolea
To give us light both good and bright with bulbs that will not blow
Oh Johnny dear, if we had it here some 50 years ago.

All the boys got jobs, they left the bogs and the turf they could not dry
To dig the holes and stand the poles, they said they'd have a try
To draw that wire through bog and mire, it was a holy show
Oh Johnny dear, if we had 'em here some 50 years ago.
We have Collins, Dan that mighty man, he drives a Bedford truck
He comes at eight, he's never late to take the boys to work
He drives so smooth till we tap the hood till we tell him to go slow.
His language then would shock old men some 50 years ago.
There's John Culnane that man of brawn from Clonakilty town
He climbs the poles with his iron soles sure he never yet fell down
He's up so high he can reach the sky and watch the sputniks glow
We had no sputniks in our skies some 50 years ago.

And there's Curley Wee he full of glee, you'll love to see him smile
A lady's man if e'er there's wan when he dresses out in style.
With his swallow tail like a coat of mail, hard hat and collar bow
Oh the girls would cheer and at him state some 50 years ago.
He's our foreman too between me and you, tis he's the right hard man
You'll have to work just like a Turk who told me, was Fat Dan
To dig the holes and stand the poles with shovel, pick and crow
They could complete no feats like these some 50 years ago.
And of all the men Con Relihan he stands out on his own
He sits upright on his tractor bright like a king upon his throne
His looks are bold like the knights of old, he dreads not friend or foe

Oh Connie there if we had you here some 50 years ago.
And in our store from Baltimore we have a senator
'Tis he no doubt will dish you out the shovel, pick and crow
To dig the holes that hold the poles with shovel pick and bar
We have the bars but no senators some 50 years ago.
We have a man that we call Tom, Tom Twomey is his name
From Millstreet town of high renown across the hills he came
He can dance and sing and in the ring he'd give you the KO
Sure he'd beat Jess Williard or Lewis as well some 50 years ago.
And our pay clerk, Ger, we call him Sir for he's a nice, smart man
We all come around each Friday when he drives up in his van
With his smiling face and attaché case pay packets filled with dough
Oh the bells would ring and we'd crown him king some 50 years ago.

*Danny Sullivan na Ceapacha is a singer and performer from Coolea,
Co Cork. His voice can be heard on his latest CD recording 'Buail Do
Phuc Is Liuigh'. Details from dannymikie@hotmail.com*

The Rural Electrification Of Carrig, 1954

Written by William Butler, Birr (RIP)
(To the air of the Mountains of Mourne)

O, Mary, this Carrig is a wonderful sight,
Where the people have in the new 'lectric light,
They don't care for tilleys or candles or lamps,
All they talk about now is their volts and their amps.
They tell me that light is a wonderful boon,
It's nearly as good as the full harvest moon,
And now you must pity a poor widow like me,
In my dark little cottage without E.S.B.
The night that the switching did gladden their hearts,
They came here to see it from arts and parts,
The supper was gorgeous as each did agree,
And everyone played with 'lectricity.
There were speeches and speeches and speeches galore,
And bould Oliver J. Sure he "took to the floor,"
And with their rejoicing, they ne'er thought of me
In my dark little cottage without E.S.B.
The farmers can now work by night and by day,
While the women can idle their whole time away,
They can plug in their kettles without any toil,
Sure in a wee minute, it's up to the boil.
For baking they tell me it's out on its own,
They just turn on a switch and leave it alone,
But I'm afraid their new gadgets will ne'er come to me
In my dark little cottage without E.S.B.

The Rural Electrification Of Carrig, 1954

I met Mickey Mooney one day in the pub,
He was drinking his pint and eating his grub,
He told me how easy life's now on the land,
You can do all the work with the switch of a hand.
You don't carry water, pulp mangels or spuds,
They've even got gadgets to wash your old duds,
May God in his goodness bring these comforts to me
In my dark little cottage without E.S.B.

About The Editors

PJ Cunningham

PJ CUNNINGHAM is an editor, publisher and journalist who is also the author of the books *The Lie of The Land*, *A Fly Never Lit* and *The Long Acre*, which was shortlisted in 2014 for Irish Book of The Year.

He also wrote *A.N. Other* in 2001 and last year was editor of the highly successful anthology on rural life – *Around The Farm Gate*.

A native of Clara, County Offaly, PJ grew up on a small farm run on horsepower and manual labour and witnessed the resistance to the new ways of tractor and electric power.

Dr Joe Kearney

DR JOE KEARNEY is a writer, broadcaster and multi-award-winning documentary maker who contributed to *Around The Farm Gate* last year. He holds a PhD in creative writing from UCD, was born and reared on the Tipperary/Kilkenny border and currently lives in County Wicklow.

Joe's early childhood was spent in a house without the benefit of Rural Electrification and his recollections of that time have informed some of his writing. His novel, *The Itinerant Beekeeper*, is due for publication in 2017.

Other publications from Ballpoint Press

AROUND *The Farm Gate* is a unique collection of stories about rural Irish life set at the crossroads between tradition and modernity in the latter part of the twentieth century.

A Fly Never Lit is the third in a trilogy of memoirs by author PJ Cunningham about rural life in Ireland from the 1960s and 1970s. It follows on from *The Lie Of The Land*, which was published in 2013, and *The Long Acre*, published in 2014, which was shortlisted for the Bord Gáis Energy Irish Book Awards for Irish Book Of The Year.

A Fly Never Lit examines the characters and events of a changing Ireland of that time. It is written with the keen perception of an eye-witness carefully watching and listening as someone clearly fascinated by the flow of 'ordinary plenty' in the daily life of rural Ireland.

To order any of the above books, visit www.ballpointpress.ie or email ballpointpress1@gmail.com